A
GREAT TRIAL
IN CHINESE HISTORY

**The Trial of the Lin Biao and Jiang Qing
Counter-Revolutionary Cliques,
Nov. 1980 — Jan. 1981**

NEW WORLD PRESS

1981

First Edition   1981

NEW WORLD PRESS
24 Baiwanzhuang Road, Beijing, China

Printed in the People's Republic of China

CONTENTS

REFLECTIONS OF A JUDGE

— By Way of a Preface

Fei Hsiao Tung*

The Standing Committee of the National People's Congress, China's highest organ of state power, decided in September last year to set up a Special Court to try the principal members of the two cliques of Lin Biao and Jiang Qing. I was asked to serve as one of the judges. It was in this capacity that I attended the trial. This has provided me with a clearer insight into the trial. At the request of the New World Press I am glad to write a preface to their new book *A Great Trial in Chinese History*. What I have put down here are some personal views and impressions which may be of some help to foreign readers who want to understand the significance of this trial.

Let me say first that the trial introduced several new features to Chinese law. The legal procedures established will be of long-term significance. One salient feature of this major trial was the clear separation of what was legally criminal from what was political.

The case before us was closely tied to a major political issue, the "cultural revolution." The crimes the defendants were accused of were committed during and under

---

* Professor Fei Hsiao Tung (Fei Xiaotong), Director of the Institute of Sociology Under the Chinese Academy of Social Sciences, is a member of the panel of judges of the Special Court.

cover of this "cultural revolution." It has been shown that the "cultural revolution" was an unmitigated disaster for the Chinese people and the wounds inflicted on the people and the nation are still raw. In order to draw lessons from it and to affix responsibilities the negative elements contributing to this disaster must be factually examined and analyzed. First of all, identify and distinguish what were errors of the political line from what were criminal violations of the law.

The gravity of the political errors of the "cultural revolution" is a known fact. As Chairman of the Standing Committee of the National People's Congress Ye Jianying said on the occasion of the 30th anniversary of the founding of the People's Republic of China in October 1979: "At the time when the cultural revolution was launched, the estimate made of the situation within the Party and the country ran counter to reality, no accurate definition was given of revisionism, and an erroneous policy and method of struggle were adopted, deviating from the principle of democratic centralism." The Chinese Communist Party is at the moment summing up the experiences since 1949 when the People's Republic was founded and drawing lessons, including the assessment of the "cultural revolution." These assessments I believe will be made public before very long.

Another major factor why the "cultural revolution" proved so destructive was because a band of scoundrels exploited the positions of power they had seized during the "cultural revolution" in an attempt to seize supreme state and Party powers by every means, legal and illegal, overt and covert, by the pen and by the gun. In the words of one of the principal accused, Zhang Chunqiao, their goal was to "supplant a dynasty." They were criminals, people who had violated the Criminal Law, and they differed fundamentally from those who had made political errors.

This analogy may be helpful. Imagine that China is a large ship advancing at high speed along a course of socialism but the navigator makes an error and the ship enters hazardous waters, where there are treacherous shoals. At this moment, some of the people in charge of the vessel clandestinely get together, form cliques, commit murder, resort to various foul means to seize the ship and turn the several hundred million on board into their slaves. Under the circumstances, the navigator must answer for his error, but his error is different in nature from those who try to exploit the navigator's error for their own despicable ends.

At the same time as the political errors of the "cultural revolution" are being summed up a step further, the criminals who had violated the law must not be allowed to escape under cover of those errors. We had been empowered by the people and in the name of the state to look into the criminal liability of the principal culprits. Those who had made mistakes of a political nature but had not violated the law did not come within our province of investigation. As to who had violated the law and who the principal culprits were, they were identified and indicted by the Special Procuratorate set up by the Standing Committee of the National People's Congress after carefully examining the case file submitted by the Ministry of Public Security. The Special Court's hearing of the indictment charging the principal culprits, and the Party's summing up its thirty years' experiences and lessons and the political assessment of the "cultural revolution" were two different things, but they were supplementary to each other.

Readers will find everywhere in this book evidence proving how Lin Biao and Jiang Qing and their cohorts had abused their positions and powers of office to do things expressly forbidden by law. Take for example the way they treated the Chairman of the People's

Republic of China Liu Shaoqi. The two cliques worked to destroy him in order to usurp Party and state powers. Liu Shaoqi, then the duly elected Chairman of the People's Republic and Vice-Chairman of the Chinese Communist Party, was ultimately persecuted to death. Jiang Qing, without a shred of evidence, publicly charged Liu Shaoqi with many crimes. She branded him an "evil man," a "thoroughly vile person" who "deserves a slow death by a thousand cuts." Her slanders were recorded and heard in court as evidence against her.

Another example. In an attempt to fabricate evidence to frame Liu Shaoqi, Jiang Qing had many people arrested and extorted confessions from them to incriminate Liu Shaoqi. She had ordered the exaction of confessions. She had not even spared an elderly man with terminal liver cancer. The hapless innocent victim was mercilessly grilled even as he was receiving glucose intravenously. His interrogators worked on him until he died. The tapes of those long hours of the interrogation under duress in his last hours were still available and were submitted before the court as evidence.

Take another example. Jiang Qing, when she was clawing her way up to become a leading power, remembered that evidence of her unsavoury past as an actress in Shanghai during the 1930's could hurt her image as "the leading proletarian revolutionary." She thereupon sent people masquerading as "Red Guards" to search and sack the homes of well-known people in the art world to find and destroy all damaging material Jiang Qing suspected were in their hands. She imprisoned many and some died in prison. One of the victims' family members appeared in court to give testimony and what she had to tell the court was profoundly moving and damning evidence against the accused.

As one who has been closely associated with the intellectual world of China for many years I know very

4

well what members of this circle had to bear. Many of them suffered terribly during those disastrous ten years. Take that famous writer Lao She for example. He was as talented, as patriotic and upright a writer as ever lived. As soon as New China was founded he returned from abroad and over the years he had written many well-known works, such as *Tea House,* which was recently presented in Western Europe where it met with a good reception. But even this patriotic writer was hounded to death by Jiang Qing.

Lin Biao, Jiang Qing and members of their cliques framed and persecuted a great number of innocent people. Their victims came from all strata of society. Leading members of the Party and the state, leading cadres and prominent intellectuals, ordinary workers, peasants and soldiers were maligned, framed and persecuted. The persecution of Shi Chuanxiang, a night-soil collector of Beijing, mentioned in the indictment against the accused is illustrative.

As everyone knows the indispensable night-soil and refuse collectors were among the lowliest and most despised in the old society. To help change this state of affairs after the founding of New China, Liu Shaoqi, the Chairman of the People's Republic, met Shi Chuanxiang and the two became friends. This was reported in the press and was widely and highly spoken of by the public. But during the "cultural revolution" the powerful Jiang Qing singled out this old worker for attack, labelling him a "scab." He was harried and died dishonoured and in great agony.

Furthermore, Lin Biao, Jiang Qing and members of their two gangs incited armed conflicts between different mass organizations. They also concocted many cases of "counter-revolutionary" organizations and groups which involved tens of thousands of people.

Take for instance the so-called "Eastern Hebei party" case. It was deliberate frame-up. Before liberation, there was a Communist Party underground organization operating in that area and its members had done much for the people and their cause. But Chen Boda, one of the most powerful men during the catastrophic period and one of the principal defendants in the trial, declared in December 1967 that this underground Party organization was "Kuomintang-controlled." He incited people to "smash up" this organization, "expose its members." This led to 84,000 innocent people being ruthlessly persecuted and the death of 2,955 persons.

In the indictment alone the accused were charged with the death of 34,800 innocent people, and the unwarranted persecution of 729,511. One foreign writer remarked that the indictment read like "a forest of names." To a foreigner it may look like that, but to us Chinese who had been through those years, it is actually "a sea of blood and tears." Shouldn't legal responsibility for their sufferings and their deaths be established?

Here, I wish to recall an old Chinese saying, "Murder on a moonless night, arson during a high wind." A dark, moonless night is a contributing condition to the murder. A moonless night does not lead to murder, nor a strong wind to arson. Neither the moon nor the wind can be held responsible for the crimes.

I must concede that as a member of the panel of judges, I had at first thought it would be very difficult to separate the errors of the "cultural revolution" from the crimes committed by Lin Biao and Jiang Qing and members of their cliques. They were so closely linked. But in the course of the trial it became quite clear that we were dealing with criminal liability, with people who had violated the Criminal Law, and not with political errors. Their offences included plotting to overthrow the government and split the state, attempting armed rebellions, having people injured or killed for counter-revolutionary ends, organizing and leading counter-revolutionary cliques, conducting demagogical propaganda for counter-revolutionary ends, torturing people to extort confessions and illegally detaining and imprisoning people. All these were clearly defined as crimes punishable by law.

It must be remarked, however, that these perpetrators of crimes in the end were given a just trial and justly adjudged by history. Some writers abroad have likened the trial to those held in Nuremberg and Tokyo after the Second World War. This is rather appropriate in my view.

The above references are to what had taken place earlier. In reference to the future, the trial is no less significant. It marks an important start being made in China to establish a complete socialist legal system. In China's long history, there have been many notorious usurpers of power who brought havoc and disaster on the country and the people. They enjoyed power for a while but their names are mentioned for ever with revulsion by the people. Some, in their lifetime, were toppled by forces of justice representing the people and justly punished. But nothing like the recent trial has ever taken place in China.

There is nothing surprising in this. Chinese society for many centuries was a feudal society and a characteristic of feudal society is government by an individual or certain individuals, and never by the law. There were laws in feudal society but the nobility was above the law. Laws were for the rulers to use against the commoners. There is an old saying which goes like this: "Beheading for stealing a coin, enthronement for stealing a state." If a poor man stole so much as a coin, he was decapitated. But if someone usurped a nation he was made a monarch!

Such a state of affairs persisted right up to the liberation of this country in 1949. From that year to 1963 more than 1,500 laws, decrees and regulations were enacted and promulgated. All of them came after the victory of the revolution and when the people wielded political power. The fundamental aim of the laws, decrees and regulations was the consolidation of what we call "people's democratic dictatorship" (i.e., the dictatorship of the proletariat) and the maintenance of socialist order. Consequently, every citizen of China, no matter who, should have abided by them. But, strictly speaking, even in that period, due to ultra-Leftism which one-sidedly stressed class struggle and the dictatorship of the proletariat, a considerable number of innocent people were branded for various alleged political crimes and without due process of law were punished. However, on the whole, China after 1949 was gradually moving towards rule by law.

But beginning in 1966, during the "cultural revolution," when nothing was allowed to remain intact, the rule of law was also demolished and lawlessness prevailed. For example, Chairman of the People's Republic Liu Shaoqi, elected by the whole people, was publicly humiliated and persecuted, ruthlessly "struggled against" with the active connivance of Jiang Qing and her cohorts. His home was violated and sacked and he was physically manhandled and violently abused and reviled. This, one must remember, took place despite the Constitution of 1954 specifically guaranteeing that the freedom of the person was inviolable and the homes of citizens of the People's Republic of China were also inviolable. His was not the only case. During those ten years of the "cultural revolution" the Constitution was ignored and the country's laws and decrees were blithely discarded and people were detained and tortured and their homes sacked.

The years of lawlessness ended with the arrest of the Gang of Four in 1976 and the whole nation began, sore at heart, quietly to review the past, firmly determined never to let such a tragedy happen again. It was recognized that socialist legality must prevail. In 1979 the National People's Congress enacted a series of important laws, including the Criminal Law of the People's Republic of China and the Law of Criminal Procedure. These came into force in 1980. Prior to this there was a nationwide movement to familiarize the people with the rule of law and impress on all that everyone is equal before the law.

This being so, the Lin Biao and Jiang Qing cliques were also charged for crimes according to the law, although everyone in China already knew that they were guilty of many heinous crimes. As a member of the panel of judges I know that from the very start of the proceedings it was particularly stressed that facts were the basis and the law was the sole criterion. This is a set principle not to be affected by feelings or other factors.

The court investigated and determined according to the law the criminal liability of the principal members of the two cliques and duly meted out punishment. At the same time the trial provided the people of the country with a lesson, vivid and profound, on the rule of law.

Because of the limited number of seats in the public gallery only some 1,200 people could attend the two Tribunals at a time. These representatives of the public came from all over the country and from every circle and every stratum, and new groups came on different days. The newspapers gave the trial extensive coverage. Some articles were quite long. The television coverage was quite extensive too. Sometimes it ran over an hour. Radio coverage was the widest, reaching a much greater public everywhere. Even those living in the most remote hamlet could follow the trial closely. The trial was followed with great interest by the public and no doubt has had a tremendous impact in a country lacking in a tradition of rule by law. More often than not, people's knowledge of trials in history was confined to what they had seen in old operas or had read in stories handed down in the centuries, where the plaintiff had to kneel before magistrates, and criminals were cangued and chained and so on. To the younger generation brought up during the "cultural revolution" on a diet of kangaroo courts, the trial had added significance. It showed that ransacking homes, beating up people, publicly humiliating people, making unfounded accusations and persecuting people were not "normal," nor "revolutionary action" as they had once been taught.

The recent trial allowed the masses of people to see for themselves what was meant by the rule of law and how trials are conducted. In China there is an old saying that "regardless of his social status, whether a prince or a commoner, a criminal is a criminal." This, in feudal society, was more a pious wish than a fact. But today people have seen this take place. No matter who he is or what high position he holds, he must be subjected to the rule of law once he violates it. Jiang Qing and other high and mighty were charged and tried according to law for crimes they had committed.

Many abroad, like the French Minister of Justice Mr. Alain Peyrefitte, have remarked that the current trial is a definite sign that China is entering a new stage of rule by the law. Of course, many abroad have also talked about the trial from the legal point of view and some have even been quite critical. I am not a jurist so I cannot join the discussion. But my jurist colleagues have expressed their views on the matter in this book. I do, however, wish to make two points. One is that we had adhered strictly to the law. The trial of the Lin-Jiang cliques is after all an affair of the Chinese, the criterion to be followed should be no other than the law of China. It would be most inappropriate to judge our legal procedure by any foreign legal system, Western or elsewhere. The second point is that, I must frankly admit, our legal system is not perfect and our experience in governing by law is rather inadequate. Still, we have made a tremendous step forward.

From a historic point of view, I see the trial as marking the formal ending to a very unfortunate period in the history of socialist China. When the Gang of Four was demolished in October 1976, the decade of chaos was swiftly terminated too. But the trial and sentencing of the accused must be seen as the formal finale to that period. In its wake a new period has appeared, a period marked by stability and unity, by democracy and the rule of law, a period in which the nation works together heart and soul for the realization of socialist modernization. We are moving forward, we are seeking a way, to building up our country of one billion people into a beautiful society. In a sense, the trial was a milestone and I am honoured to have had the opportunity to serve in this historic trial. I am pleased to see that the New World Press is bringing out this book for readers abroad. It is a worthy endeavour that I have been asked to write a preface for.

January 1981

FROM INDICTMENT TO TRIAL

The People's Courts administer justice independently, subject only to the law.

Article 4 of the *Organic Law of the People's Courts**

In judicial proceedings in the people's courts, the law is applied equally to all citizens, irrespective of nationality, race, sex, occupation, social origin, religious belief, education, property status, or length of residence. No privilege is allowed.

Article 5 of the *Organic Law of the People's Courts*

All cases in the people's courts are heard in public except those involving state secrets, personal shameful secrets and juvenile delinquencies.

Article 7 of the *Organic Law of the People's Courts*

The Supreme People's Court has a criminal division, a civil division, an economic division and such other divisions as are deemed necessary.

Article 31 of the *Organic Law of the People's Courts*

. . . .

The President of the Supreme People's Court is elected by the National People's Congress; Vice-Presidents, chief judges of divisions, associate chief judges of divisions and judges are appointed and removed by the Standing Committee of the National People's Congress.

Article 35 of the *Organic Law of the People's Courts*

---

* Translations of all quoted matter from the *Criminal Law*, the *Law of Criminal Procedure* and the *Organic Law of the People's Courts*, of the People's Republic of China, are ours. — *Ed.*

Where the People's Procuratorate holds that the facts of the offence of the accused have been ascertained, the evidence is valid and ample and the criminal liability shall be pursued according to law, it shall make a decision of preferring a charge and, in accordange with the provisions regarding jurisdiction, prefer a public charge to a competent people's court.

Article 100 of the *Law of Criminal Procedure*

. . . serve on the accused a copy of the charge sheet of the People's Procuratorate by not less than seven days prior to the opening of the court session, and inform the accused that he may call in an advocate, or, where necessary, designate an advocate on his behalf.

Item 2, Article 110 of the *Law of Criminal Procedure*

SPECIAL PROCURATORATE AND SPECIAL COURT SET UP

On September 29, 1980, the Standing Committee of the Fifth National People's Congress (N.P.C.) established a Special Procuratorate and Special Court to prosecute and try the principal members of the counter-revolutionary cliques of Lin Biao and Jiang Qing. The popularly elected National People's Congress is China's supreme organ of state power and law-making body.

The ten principal defendants prosecuted in the case were Jiang Qing, Zhang Chunqiao, Yao Wenyuan, Wang Hongwen, Chen Boda, Huang Yongsheng, Wu Faxian, Li Zuopeng, Qiu Huizuo and Jiang Tengjiao. As the provisions of Item 5, Article 11 of China's Law of Criminal Procedure exempt defendants who are dead from prosecution for their crimes, no proceedings were taken to attach criminal responsibility to the six deceased principal

13

defendants — Lin Biao, Kang Sheng, Xie Fuzhi, Ye Qun, Lin Liguo, and Zhou Yuchi (see p. 30 for full list of the 16 principal accused and the posts they had formerly held).

It was made clear at the N.P.C. Standing Committee meeting that the charges against the two cliques would involve only counter-revolutionary violations of the Criminal Law, and not errors in work, including those related to political line.

Huang Huoqing, Chief Procurator of China's Supreme People's Procuratorate, was appointed Chief of the Special Procuratorate, and Jiang Hua, President of China's Supreme People's Court, was appointed President of the Special Court.

The Special Court consisted of two Tribunals. Zeng Hanzhou, Vice-President of the Supreme People's Court, was named to preside over the First Tribunal while Wu Xiuquan, Deputy Chief of the General Staff of the People's Liberation Army, was appointed chief judge of the Second Tribunal. Other members of the Special Procuratorate and the Special Court were also appointed (see lists on pp. 15-17).

The National People's Congress Standing Committee decided that the Special Court would conduct open trials and its judgement would be final.

COMPOSITION OF THE SPECIAL PROCURATORATE

Chief Procurator:
  Huang Huoqing (Huang Huo-ching 黄火青)
Deputy Chief Procurators:
  Yu Ping (Yu Ping 喻　屏)
  Shi Jinqian (Shi Chin-chien 史进前)
Procurators (*in alphabetical order*):
  Feng Changyi (Feng Chang-i 冯长义)
  Jiang Wen (Chiang Wen 江　文)
  Jing Yusong (Ching Yu-sung 敬毓嵩)
  Li Tianxiang (Li Tien-hsiang 李天相)
  Ma Chunyi (Ma Chun-i 马纯一)
  Meng Qingen (Meng Ching-en 孟庆恩)
  Qu Wenda (Chu Wen-ta 曲文达)
  Shen Jialiang (Shen Chia-liang 沈家良)
  Sun Shufeng (Sun Shu-feng 孙树峰)
  Tu Men (Tu Men 图　们)
  Wang Fang (Wang Fang 王　芳)
  Wang Pusheng (Wang Pu-sheng 王瀑声)
  Wang Wenlin (Wang Wen-lin 王文林)
  Wang Yaoqing (Wang Yao-ching 王耀青) (female)
  Wang Zhenzhong (Wang Chen-chung 王振中)
  Yuan Tongjiang (Yuan Tung-chiang 袁同江)
  Zhang Zhaoqi (Chang Chao-chi 张肇圻)
  Zhang Yingjie (Chang Ying-chieh 张英杰)
  Zhang Zhongru (Chang Chung-ju 张中如)
  Zhong Shuqin (Chong Shu-chin 钟澍钦)
  Zhu Zongzheng (Chu Chung-cheng 朱宗正)

COMPOSITION OF THE SPECIAL COURT

President: Jiang Hua (Chiang Hua 江　华)

Vice-Presidents: Wu Xiuquan (Wu Hsiu-chuan 伍修权)
Zeng Hanzhou (Tseng Han-chou 曾汉周)
Huang Yukun (Huang Yu-kun　黄玉昆)

Chief Judge of the First Tribunal:
Zeng Hanzhou (Tseng Han-chou 曾汉周)

Chief Judge of the Second Tribunal:
Wu Xiuquan (Wu Hsiu-chuan 伍修权)

Judges (*in alphabetical order*):
Cao Lizhou (Tsao Li-chou 曹理周)
Fan Zhi (Fan Chih 范　之)
Fei Xiaotong (Fei Hsiao Tung 费孝通)
Gan Ying (Kan Ying 甘　英) (female)
Gao Bin (Kao Pin 高　斌)
Gao Chaoxun (Kao Chao-hsun 高朝勋)
Huang Liangchen (Huang Liang-chen　黄凉尘)
Li Yi (Li I 李　毅)
Li Minggui (Li Ming-kuei　李明贵)
Liu Jiguang (Liu Chi-kuang　刘继光)
Liu Liying (Liu Li-ying　刘丽英) (female)
Lo Tongqi (Lo Tung-chi　骆同启)
Ning Huanxing (Ning Huan-hsing　宁焕星)
Qu Yucai (Chu Yu-tsai　曲育才)
Ren Chenghong (Jen Cheng-hung　任成宏)
Ren Lingyun (Jen Ling-yun　任凌云)

Shen Jian (Shen Chien 沈　建)

Shi Xiaotan (Shi Hsiao-tan 史笑谈)

Situ Jing (Situ Ching 司徒擎)

Su Ziheng (Su Tsu-heng 苏子蘅)

Wang Wenzheng (Wang Wen-cheng 王文正)

Wang Zhanping (Wang Chan-ping 王战平)

Wang Zhidao (Wang Chih-tao 王志道)

Wu Baosan (Wu Pao-san 巫宝三)

Wu Maosun (Wu Mao-sun 吴茂荪)

Xu Zongqi (Hsu Tsung-chi 许宗祺)

Yan Xinmin (Yan Hsin-min 严信民)

Zhai Xuexi (Chai Hsueh-hsi 翟学玺)

Zhang Min (Chang Min 张　敏)

Zhang Shirong (Chang Shi-jung 张世荣)

Zhu Lizhi (Chu Li-chih 朱理之)

FOUR MAJOR CHARGES

Based on the investigation carried out since April 1980 by the Ministry of Public Security and after interrogating the accused, the Special Procuratorate drew up an indictment.* On November 10, copies of this indictment citing 48 specific offences were served on Jiang Qing and the nine other accused. The two counter-revolutionary cliques were charged with four major crimes:

• Framing and persecuting Party and state leaders and plotting to overthrow the political power of the dictatorship of the proletariat;

• Persecuting and suppressing large numbers of cadres and ordinary people;

• Plotting to assassinate Chairman Mao Zedong and to stage an armed counter-revolutionary coup d'etat; and

• Plotting an armed rebellion in Shanghai.

Here are some main points of the indictment.

Persecution of Party and State Leaders

The Lin-Jiang cliques framed and persecuted Liu Shaoqi, Chairman of the People's Republic of China and Vice-Chairman of the Central Committee of the Chinese Communist Party; Zhou Enlai, Vice-Chairman of the C.P.C. Central Committee and Premier of the State Council; Zhu De, Vice-Chairman of the C.P.C. Central Committee and Chairman of the Standing Committee of the

---

* See page 149 for the full text of the indictment.

National People's Congress; Deng Xiaoping, Member of the Standing Committee of the Political Bureau, General Secretary of the C.P.C. Central Committee and Vice-Premier of the State Council, and a number of other leading members of the Party and the state.

In August 1966, Lin Biao and his wife, Ye Qun, made false charges against Liu Shaoqi. Ye Qun dictated these trumped-up charges to an army officer and ordered him to put them into writing, which Lin Biao read and approved. He told the officer that he should write an accompanying letter addressed to Lin Biao and Chairman Mao Zedong. Lin Biao then gave the letter and the fabricated material to Jiang Qing to be forwarded to Chairman Mao.

In July 1967, Jiang Qing, Kang Sheng and Chen Boda approved the holding of a "rally for repudiating and struggling against Liu Shaoqi." At the rally, Liu Shaoqi and his wife, Wang Guangmei, were reviled and manhandled and their house was searched and ransacked.

In July and August of the same year, Kang Sheng, Xie Fuzhi and their followers incited certain persons to set up an organization, which called itself a "frontline for getting Liu Shaoqi out of Zhongnanhai,*" to besiege the official residence of Liu Shaoqi on the premises of the State Council and to storm it.

Jiang Qing had direct control of the "group for investigating into the special case of Liu Shaoqi and Wang Guangmei" and directed its work in collusion with Kang Sheng and Xie Fuzhi. Jiang Qing had eleven people unlawfully arrested, imprisoned, then interrogated and tortured to extort confessions and rig up "evidence" vilifying Liu Shaoqi and his wife as "renegades," "enemy agents" and "counter-revolutionaries."

Premier Zhou Enlai and other leaders were also falsely

---

* The site of the Party Centre and the State Council.

THE GRIM STATISTICS

The Indictment mentions by name 420 victims of frame-ups and persecution. Among them:

- 38 leaders of the Party and State;

- 93 members and alternate members of the Central Committee of the Chinese Communist Party and 30 members and alternate members of its Control Commission;

- 36 members of the Standing Committee of the National People's Congress;

- 47 members of the Standing Committee of the National Committee of the Chinese People's Political Consultative Conference;

- 84 high-ranking cadres of the Party, State and Army;

- 19 leading members of various democratic parties;

- 37 other well-known personages in various fields; and

- 36 others.

A total of 729,511 people were framed and persecuted in cases mentioned in the Indictment, of whom 34,800 were persecuted to death.

---

charged by Jiang Qing and her Gang. Wang Hongwen was sent with malicious intent to Changsha in October 1974 to persuade Chairman Mao Zedong that Zhou Enlai, Deng Xiaoping and others were "plotting" to usurp power. The gang also made use of the media under their control to stir up a nationwide campaign to criticize the "big Confucianist of our time" and the "Chief Minister," to attack Zhou Enlai by innuendo.

	Number of people framed and persecuted	Number of people persecuted to death
The eastern Hebei case	84,000	2,955
The case of "enemy agent Zhao Jianmin" in Yunnan		14,000
The case of the "Inner Mongolian people's revolutionary party"	346,000	16,222
The case of "Xinjiang renegade clique"	92	26
The case of the "counter-revolutionary northeast gang that betrayed the Party and capitulated to the enemy"	90	4
The case of the "Guangdong underground Party organization"	7,100	85
Cases of the P.L.A.	80,000	1,169
The violent incidents in Shanghai	741	
The Jinan incident	388	
Leading members of democratic parties		18
Personages in various circles	211,100	40
Returned overseas Chinese		281
Total	**729,511**	**34,800**

Reprinted from China Reconstructs, *No. 2, 1981*

Jiang Qing, Zhang Chunqiao and Yao Wenyuan libellously charged that Deng Xiaoping was a "counter-revolutionary double-dealer," "general manager of a rumour-mongering company," a "fascist," a "big quisling," and a "representative of the comprador bourgeoisie."

Chen Boda, Xie Fuzhi and Wu Faxian made use of the case of the "Extraordinary Central Committee of the Communist Party of China" leaflet uncovered in Tianjin in November 1967 to cook up a case involving a non-existent "Chinese Communist Party (M-L)" and asserted that Zhu De was "secretary" of the alleged Party Central Committee.

On July 21, 1968, Kang Sheng sent a confidential letter to Jiang Qing. In this letter, he wrote, "Enclosed please find the list of names you asked for." On this list drawn up by Kang Sheng and in his own handwriting, he labelled 88 of the 193 Members and Alternate Members of the Eighth C.P.C. Central Committee as "enemy agents," "renegades," "elements having illicit relations with foreign countries" or "anti-Party elements."

Kang Sheng also instructed the person in charge of the Organization Department of the Party Central Committee to level false charges against 171 persons in leading positions in the Party Central Committee's Control Commission, the National People's Congress and the Chinese People's Political Consultative Conference (C.P.P.C.C. is a united front organization).

Inciting Violence

Another charge against the Lin-Jiang cliques was inciting a wave of "beating, smashing and looting," which led to nationwide violence all over China during the "cultural revolution."

To crush a mass organization in Shanghai known as the "Workers' Red Detachment," Zhang Chunqiao instructed Wang Hongwen in December 1966 to work with some smash-and-looters and incite people ignorant of the real situation to attack the "Detachment." This armed clash, known as the Kangping Road Incident, resulted in 91 people being seriously wounded.

In August 1967, Wang Hongwen engineered and directed an armed attack on a mass organization known as the

"Rebel Headquarters of the Revolutionary Alliance of the Shanghai Diesel Engine Plant." At least 650 people were gravely wounded and jailed.

Zhang Chunqiao and Yao Wenyuan abetted the violence in the compound of the Shandong Provincial Revolutionary Committee in May 1967, in which 388 persons were arrested and imprisoned.

Through Wu Faxian and in collaboration with Lin Biao's wife, Ye Qun, Jiang Qing in October 1966 ordered more than 40 people disguised as red guards to search and ransack the homes of five film and opera artists in Shanghai. The pretext was that they had in their hands a certain letter* by Jiang Qing. The material taken away by the raiders were later burnt under Jiang Qing's personal supervision by Xie Fuzhi and Ye Qun.

Zhang Chunqiao directed in Shanghai a clandestine counter-revolutionary detachment known as the "You Xuetao Group." This group carried out such special tasks as surveillance, kidnapping, ransacking homes, seizing people, secret interrogations and torture and gathering intelligence.

Framing Innocent People

The Lin-Jiang cliques framed and harmed a shocking number of people throughout the country.

Here are some of the major frame-ups:

The Eastern Hebei Case: In December 1967, Chen Boda groundlessly charged that the Communist Party organization in eastern Hebei was "probably a Party of Kuomintang-Communist co-operation," in which the Kuomintang and renegades played the dominant role. As a result, more

---

* The five had known Jiang Qing as an actress under the name of Lan Ping. And certain things she had done in the thirties would not redound to her credit if publicized.

than 84,000 Party cadres and other people in that area were framed and persecuted, and 2,955 died unnatural deaths.

The "Enemy Agent Zhao Jianmin" case: In January 1968, Kang Sheng and Xie Fuzhi charged that Zhao Jianmin, secretary of the C.P.C. Yunnan Provincial Committee, was a "renegade" and falsely accused him of "working for a group of Kuomintang agents in Yunnan." This led to the persecution of large numbers of cadres and ordinary people in that province, over 14,000 of whom died as a result.

The case of the "Inner Mongolian People's Revolutionary Party": This and other false cases concocted in the Inner Mongolian Autonomous Region at the instigation of Kang Sheng and Xie Fuzhi resulted in the framing and persecution of more than 346,000 cadres and other people, 16,222 of whom died as a result.

Plot to Assassinate Chairman Mao and Stage an Armed Coup

Lin Biao, after his bid to become chairman of the state and usurp power by a "peaceful transition" failed, put into motion a plot for an armed counter-revolutionary coup d'etat.

In February 1971, Lin Biao and Ye Qun sent their son, Lin Liguo, to Shanghai, where he called together key members of the "Joint Fleet" — as they described their counter-revolutionary special detachment — to work out details of the coup. The blueprint for the coup was called *Outline for "Project 571."* ("571" being a pun on the Chinese for "armed uprising" — Ed.)

Under the direct leadership of Lin Biao, Lin Liguo assigned Jiang Tengjiao to be "frontline commander" for action in the Shanghai area. Their plans included attacking Chairman Mao's special train with flame throwers and 40-mm. rocket-guns, dynamiting the Shuofang railway bridge near Suzhou, over which the train was to pass, bombing the train from the air, etc.

When Lin Biao and Ye Qun learned on the evening of September 11 that their plot to assassinate Chairman Mao had fallen through and that the Chairman had already left Shanghai for Beijing, the two decided to fly south to Guangzhou with their collaborators to set up a separate "party central committee" there and split the nation. They even plotted "a pincer attack from north and south in alliance with the Soviet Union."

A special plane was sent with Lin Liguo on board to a place close to the summer resort of Beidaihe for Lin Biao and Ye Qun to fly south. Late in the night of September 12, Lin Biao and his wife and son learned from their secret source that Premier Zhou Enlai had been making inquiries about the unauthorized sending of the special plane. The Lins hurriedly took off at 00:32 hours on September 13 for a foreign country. The plane crashed on the way. The wreckage and the bodies of all on board were found near Undur Khan in Mongolia.

Armed Rebellion Plotted in Shanghai

In July 1967, Zhang Chunqiao instructed Wang Hongwen and others to organize an armed force under their control in Shanghai. Between 1973-76, Wang Hongwen said to his followers on several occasions: "What worries me most is that the army is not in our hands." He told them to keep command of the Shanghai militia in their hands and said that he himself would take charge of it.

By September 1976, Shanghai's militiamen were armed with 74,000 rifles, 300 artillery pieces and more than 10 million rounds of ammunition. Zhang Chunqiao in Beijing was kept informed of the situation. Zhang himself gave top directives.

On October 6, 1976, in Beijing, the Gang of Four — Jiang Qing, Zhang Chunqiao, Yao Wenyuan and Wang Hongwen — were taken into custody. Upon learning this on October 8 through a prearranged secret code, co-conspirators in Shanghai immediately called an emergency meeting and decided to use the militia for an armed rebellion. But the plot failed.

———————◆———————

DEFENCE LAWYERS

On November 10, when copies of the indictment of the Special Procuratorate were served on Jiang Qing and the nine other accused, the Special Court, in accordance with the provisions on the right to defence stipulated in the Law of Criminal Procedure, informed them that they had the right to defend themselves or entrust their defence to advocates.

Chen Boda, Wu Faxian, Li Zuopeng and Jiang Tengjiao turned in applications requesting to retain lawyers, and Yao Wenyuan preferred the court to assign lawyers for him. The Special Court recommended a number of experienced lawyers from Beijing, Shanghai, Wuhan and Xi'an, some of whom have had more than 50 years of judicial experience. From November 13 on, the defence lawyers met with and consulted with the accused.

Jiang Qing at first requested lawyers for her defence, and the Special Court recommended three lawyers on two occasions. In her interviews with the lawyers, Jiang Qing demanded that they speak in her behalf and answer questions in her stead in court. The lawyers rejected her demands which contradict the law, telling her that the responsibility of the defence lawyer was to safeguard the legitimate rights and interests of the accused according to facts and law, and not to act as the defendant's mouthpiece and answer questions the court addressed to her. Jiang Qing then said she did not need defence lawyers.

The four other defendants in the case did not apply for defence counsel.

LIST OF DEFENCE LAWYERS

Defence Lawyers	Defendants
Gan Yupei (Kan Yu-pei 甘雨霈) Lawyer, Associate Professor of Law at Beijing University	Chen Boda （陈伯达）
Fu Zhiren (Fu Chih-jen 傅志人) Secretary General of the Beijing Lawyers' Association	
Ma Kechang (Ma Ke-chang 马克昌) Lawyer, Associate Professor of Law at Wuhan University	Wu Faxian （吴法宪）
Zhou Hengyuan (Chou Heng-yuan 周亨元) Lawyer, Lecturer of Law at the China People's University	

Zhang Sizhi
(Chang Si-chih　张思之)

Li Zuopeng
(李作鹏)

　　Vice-President of the Beijing
　　Lawyers' Association

Su Huiyu
(Su Hui-yu　苏惠渔)

　　Lawyer, Lecturer at the East
　　China Institute of Political
　　Science and Law

Wang Shunhua
(Wang Shun-hua　王舜华)

Jiang Tengjiao
(江腾蛟)

　　Lawyer, Assistant Research
　　Fellow at the Law Institute
　　Under the Chinese Academy
　　of Social Sciences

Zhou Kuizheng
(Chou Kwei-cheng　周奎正)

　　Leading Member of the Beijing
　　Lawyers' Association

Han Xuezhang
(Han Hsieh-chang　韩学章)(female)

Yao Wenyuan
(姚文元)

　　Vice-President of the Shanghai
　　Lawyers' Association

Zhang Zhong
(Chang Chong　张　中)

　　Lawyer of the Shanghai Lawyers'
　　Association

THE TRIAL BEGINS

On November 20, 1980, the historic trial began. The court met at No. 1 Zhengyi (Justice) Road, Beijing.

After Jiang Hua, President of the Special Court, declared the court in session at 15:00 Beijing time, bailiffs led Jiang Qing and the nine other defendants to the dock.

Huang Huoqing, Chief Procurator of the Special Procuratorate, read out the indictment.

President Jiang Hua then declared that the ten defendants would stand trial in the First and Second Tribunals in two separate groups. The defendants to be tried by the First Tribunal were Jiang Qing, Zhang Chunqiao, Yao Wenyuan, Wang Hongwen and Chen Boda. The defendants to be tried by the Second Tribunal were Huang Yongsheng, Wu Faxian, Li Zuopeng, Qiu Huizuo and Jiang Tengjiao.

President Jiang Hua addressing the defendants said that they must abide by the orders of the court in the proceedings and not violate its rules and regulations. He also told them that they had the right to defence and that the right to speak last at the end of the trial was theirs.

In the public gallery of the Special Court were representatives from various provinces, autonomous regions and municipalities, departments under the Central Committee of the Communist Party of China, state organs, people's organizations, democratic parties and the Chinese People's Liberation Army. Many of the representatives had been framed and persecuted by Lin Biao, Jiang Qing and other members of the two cliques.

China Central Television televised parts of the trial to the rest of the world via satellite.

Court investigation of the charges began on November 23 and debate ended on December 29. Altogether 20 sessions were held by the First Tribunal and 22 by the Second.

Principal Members of the Lin Biao and Jiang Qing Counter-Revolutionary Cliques

(In alphabetical order)

Chen Boda (Chen Po-ta 陈伯达)
Member of the Ninth Central Committee of the Chinese Communist Party (C.P.C.), its Political Bureau and the Bureau's Standing Committee.

Huang Yongsheng (Huang Yung-sheng 黄永胜)
Member of the Ninth Central Committee of the C.P.C. and its Political Bureau and chief of the General Staff of the Chinese People's Liberation Army (P.L.A.).

Jiang Qing (Chiang Ching 江 青)
Member of the Tenth Central Committee of the C.P.C. and its Political Bureau.

Jiang Tengjiao (Chiang Teng-chiao 江腾蛟)
Air Force political commissar of the P.L.A. Nanjing Units.

Kang Sheng (Kang Sheng 康 生 — now dead)
Vice-Chairman of the Tenth Central Committee of the C.P.C.

Li Zuopeng (Li Tso-peng 李作鹏)
Member of the Ninth Central Committee of the C.P.C. and its Political Bureau, and deputy chief of the P.L.A. General Staff and concurrently first political commissar of the P.L.A. Navy.

Lin Biao (Lin Piao 林 彪 — now dead)
Vice-Chairman of the Ninth Central Committee of the C.P.C., Vice-Chairman of the Military Commission of the C.P.C. Central Committee, and Minister of National Defence.

Lin Liguo (Lin Li-kuo 林立果 — now dead)
Son of Lin Biao. Deputy director of the General Office and concurrently deputy chief of the Operations Department of the Air Force Command.

Qiu Huizuo (Chiu Hui-tso 邱会作)
Member of the Ninth Central Committee of the C.P.C. and its Political Bureau. Deputy chief of the P.L.A. General Staff and concurrently director of the P.L.A. General Logistics Department.

Wang Hongwen (Wang Hung-wen 王洪文)
Vice-Chairman of the Tenth Central Committee of the C.P.C., secretary of the Shanghai Municipal Committee of the C.P.C. and vice-chairman of the Shanghai Municipal Revolutionary Committee.

Wu Faxian (Wu Fa-hsien 吴法宪)
Member of the Ninth Central Committee of the C.P.C. and its Political Bureau, deputy chief of the P.L.A. General Staff and concurrently commander of the P.L.A. Air Force.

Yao Wenyuan (Yao Wen-yuan 姚文元)
Member of the Tenth Central Committee of the C.P.C. and its Political Bureau, second secretary of the Shanghai Municipal Committee of the C.P.C. and vice-chairman of the Shanghai Municipal Revolutionary Committee.

Ye Qun (Yeh Chun 叶 群 — now dead)
Wife of Lin Biao. Member of the Political Bureau of the Ninth Central Committee of the C.P.C.

Xie Fuzhi (Hsieh Fu-chih 谢富治 — now dead)
Member of the Political Bureau of the Ninth Central Committee of the C.P.C., Vice-Premier of the State Council and Minister of Public Security.

31

Zhang Chunqiao (Chang Chun-chiao 张春桥)
Member of the Tenth Central Committee of the C.P.C.,
its Political Bureau and the Bureau's Standing Committee, Vice-Premier of the State Council, director of
the General Political Department of the P.L.A., first
secretary of the Shanghai Municipal Committee of the
C.P.C. and chairman of the Shanghai Municipal Revolutionary Committee.

Zhou Yuchi (Chou Yu-chih 周宇驰 — now dead)
Deputy director of the General Office of the Air Force
Command.

HIGHLIGHTS OF COURT INVESTIGATION

. . . .

No evidence shall serve as the basis of a judgement before it has been ascertained and verified.

Article 31 of the *Law of Criminal Procedure*

Stress should be laid on evidence, investigation and studies, and one should not be too ready to believe the confession of an accused. No accused shall be adjudged guilty and sentenced without evidence other than his confession; he shall be convicted and punished if there is sufficient evidence against him even without his confession.

Article 8 of the *Law of Criminal Procedure*

THE FRAMING AND PERSECUTION OF STATE CHAIRMAN LIU SHAOQI

Lin Biao, Jiang Qing and their accomplices regarded Liu Shaoqi and other Party and state leaders as their biggest obstacles to usurping Party leadership and state power, so they used intrigues to frame and to destroy them. Liu Shaoqi, Chairman of the People's Republic and Vice-Chairman of the Central Committee of the C.P.C., was persecuted to death in 1969. He was rehabilitated posthumously in 1980 after thoroughgoing re-investigation.

From November 27 to December 5, the First Tribunal investigated facts concerning the frame-up of Liu Shaoqi. Following are some highlights of the court hearings.

Lei Yingfu's Notes

The prosecution introduced as evidence Lei Yingfu's notes, the text of a letter and other material proving Jiang Qing's collaboration with Lin Biao in trumping up charges against Liu Shaoqi. Lei was Deputy Director of the Operations Department of the Headquarters of the General Staff of the People's Liberation Army.

According to Lei's notes and other material, Ye Qun, Lin Biao's wife, summoned Lei Yingfu, on August 11 and 12, and dictated to him 13 charges against Liu and Deng Xiaoping. Ye Qun instructed him to commit these charges to writing. One sentence in Lei's notes read: "Ye said that the above were what 101 (Lin Biao's code number) told her to tell me." Lin Biao's accusations against Liu Shaoqi, as dictated by Ye Qun, and recorded in Lei's notes, included: "He (Liu) wants to become the supreme commander"; "He is building up an independent kingdom"; "He has shielded bad elements like Peng Zhen (former Mayor of Beijing) and Luo Ruiqing (former Chief of General Staff of the P.L.A., now dead)."

The notes also showed that Lin Biao made other accusations, through Ye Qun, implying that there was collusion between Liu Shaoqi, Deng Xiaoping and Marshal He Long (now dead). Lin said that Chairman Mao should be warned that "Liu Shaoqi and Deng Xiaoping are trying to pull He Long over to their side."

Lei's notes showed that Lin Biao summoned him to his residence on August 14, 1966. The entry read: "Today, at Commander Lin's residence, he told me that I should write up the material and enclose it in a letter addressed to Lin Biao and Chairman Mao Zedong. He would then forward it to the Chairman. This way, it would appear more political."

Lei did as he was told and Lin Biao sent the letter off to Jiang Qing on that very day with this accompanying note: "Comrade Jiang Qing, please read and forward it to the Chairman if you see fit."

Kuai Dafu's Testimony

On November 27, the First Tribunal investigated the charge that Zhang Chunqiao incited Kuai Dafu (one of the leaders of the Beijing student "rebels") to agitate publicly for the overthrow of Liu Shaoqi and Deng Xiaoping.

The judge questioned Zhang Chunqiao as to whether he had incited Kuai. Zhang refused to answer. The judge then summoned Kuai Dafu (now in custody) to appear in court to give testimony. Kuai admitted that on December 18, 1966, Zhang Chunqiao received him privately in a reception room at Zhongnanhai (site of the Party Centre and the State Council) and directed him "unmistakably and clearly" to publicly discredit Liu Shaoqi and Deng Xiaoping. Kuai said that Zhang told him: "Those two in the Central Committee who put forward the reactionary bourgeois line have not yet surrendered. . . . You young revolutionary fighters should unite, carry forward your thoroughgoing revolutionary spirit and flog the cur that has fallen into the water. Make their very names stink. Don't stop half way." Kuai said: "Zhang Chunqiao, as a deputy leader of the Cultural Revolution Group Under the C.P.C. Central Committee, received me privately and put all his cards on the table, which, I thought, was a show of special trust in me." This conversation led Kuai to organizing a demonstration in Beijing on December 25, 1966, with 5,000 demonstrators shouting the slogans, "Down with Liu Shaoqi" and "Down with Deng Xiaoping." The demonstrators plastered the city with big character posters and passed out huge numbers of leaflets vilifying Liu and Deng. This was followed by mounting a campaign throughout the country to overthrow Liu and Deng. Kuai said: "Zhang Chunqiao played the role of behind-the-scene manipulator throughout the whole business of us opposing Comrades Liu Shaoqi and Deng Xiaoping."

Zhang Chunqiao said nothing throughout the whole session.

Illegal Search of the State Chairman's Home

During the court's investigation of November 28, Chen Boda, one of the ten principal culprits, said he could not recall that in July 1967 he, together with Jiang Qing and Kang Sheng, had approved the holding of a meeting to struggle against Liu Shaoqi.

The court then read out a deposition by Qi Benyu (a member of the Cultural Revolution Group Under the C.P.C. Central Committee). Qi declared that in a report (see p. 4 of pictorial section) submitted by him to Jiang Qing, Kang Sheng and Chen Boda, in which he asked for permission to organize a "rally to repudiate and struggle against Liu Shaoqi," Chen Boda changed "Liu Shaoqi" in the report to "Liu, Deng, Tao and their wives," thus enlarging the number of persons to be denounced from one to six. (Deng and Tao refer to Deng Xiaoping and Tao Zhu. Both were Vice-Premiers of the State Council and Members of the Standing Committee of the Party's Political Bureau.)

When the court showed the defendant, Chen Boda, a photocopy of the report referred to in the deposition, Chen admitted that the changed words were in his handwriting and that he now remembered sanctioning the rally in question.

Qi Benyu's deposition also stated: "Before taking action, I asked Jiang Qing whether she should cable the Chairman

(Chairman Mao, not in Beijing at that time) and ask his permission. Jiang Qing told me not to bother. She would do the cabling." Jiang Qing did not send the cable.

On the night of July 18, 1967, a horde of people broke into Liu Shaoqi's home and dragged him and his wife Wang Guangmei to two separate halls in Zhongnanhai where they were subjected to insults and humiliation for two hours and 20 minutes. The State Chairman's home was searched and ransacked.

Following this, said the prosecution, the cry "Down with Liu, Deng and Tao" was spread to all China. Thousands upon thousands of innocent people were labelled "agents" or "lackeys of Liu, Deng and Tao," and were publicly abused and humiliated, tortured and persecuted. Party and government organizations throughout China were paralyzed. Liu Shaoqi and Wang Guangmei were placed under house arrest after their home was raided on July 18. A few days later, both Deng Xiaoping and Tao Zhu and their wives were also deprived of their freedom of movement.

At a court session on December 5, when Jiang Qing was questioned about the charge that she had approved the illegal struggle meeting against Liu Shaoqi, she said that she had no recollection of it. When evidence was shown that she had indeed approved it, she admitted the charge, but said that her actions — approving the illegal struggle meeting and the raid on Liu Shaoqi's residence — were "justifiable and lawful" and, therefore "did not constitute a criminal offence." Jiang Qing also claimed that the Decision Concerning the Great Cultural Revolution adopted at the 11th Plenary Session of the Eighth Party Central Committee in 1966 approved actions against the "four olds" (namely, old ideas, old culture, old customs and old habits). "Doing away with the four olds would inevitably call for the searching of houses, which was a revolutionary action," she argued.

The prosecution rebutted Jiang Qing's claim, pointing out that not one of the 16 articles in the said Decision provided grounds for repudiating and struggling against the State Chairman and searching and ransacking his official residence. Criminal liability must be borne by the accused, Jiang Qing, he declared.

Huang Huoqing, Chief of the Special Procuratorate, pointed out that under Article 36 of the Organic Law of the National People's Congress adopted in 1954, N.P.C. deputies are immune from arrest or trial without a decision by the N.P.C. or its Standing Committee when the N.P.C. is not in session. "This being the case, what right had Jiang Qing and others to instigate and approve a meeting to denounce and struggle against the State Chairman, an official elected by the N.P.C.? It was in distinct contravention of the law," he stated.

Jiang Qing Controls the Case Against Liu Shaoqi

Earlier, at the December 3 court hearing, Jiang Qing denied the charges in the indictment that she directly controlled the "group for investigating into the special case of Liu Shaoqi and Wang Guangmei" and that she had directed its work together with Kang Sheng and Xie Fuzhi, both powerful figures at that time.

Among relevant documentary and testimonial evidence produced was a directive written by Xie Fuzhi on February 26, 1968 on a report submitted by the special group handling the case, which stated: "The main work concerning the case of the big renegade, Liu Shaoqi, is under Comrade Jiang Qing's personal control. From now on, all reports on important issues and those asking for instructions should first be submitted directly to Comrade Jiang Qing."

According to evidence submitted by the prosecution, Jiang Qing, on June 26, 1968, was incensed that the special group had submitted to her only abridged versions of documents. She wrote to the group complaining that their failure to give her the full original material smacked of "usurping" her power. "If I have not fulfilled my duty, or I have committed a grave error, remove me from my post." If not, then "you must make a self-criticism and seriously correct your mistakes." Thereupon, two leading members of the special group, Wang Dongxing and Xie Fuzhi, hastily submitted a written self-criticism.

The court heard a recording of Jiang Qing addressing a public meeting on September 18, 1968. In the speech she said: "I am in charge of the first big special case. . . . Now, let me tell you, Liu Shaoqi is a big counter-revolutionary, a big hidden traitor, a big renegade and big enemy agent, full of evil. . . . I think he deserves a slow death by a thousand cuts, ten thousand cuts. . . ."

The evidence was overwhelming and Jiang Qing had to admit that she had been in direct charge of the special group handling the case.

Jiang Qing's Order for the Arrest of Liu Shaoqi's Wife

The court heard on December 3 the charge that Jiang Qing and Kang Sheng instigated the framing and arrest of Liu Shaoqi's wife, Wang Guangmei, as an agent of the U.S. strategic intelligence service. Testimony was given by Xiao Meng, who once headed the "group for investigating into the special case of Liu Shaoqi and Wang Guangmei."

Xiao Meng testified that between May and November 1967, he headed the special group. On the evening of September 3, 1967, he said, Kang Sheng summoned him by phone to Diao Yu Tai (the state guest house in Beijing). Xiao Meng was met by Kang Sheng and Jiang Qing, no one else was present. "Tonight, your special group must write a report requesting permission to arrest Wang Guangmei. Hand me the report tomorrow morning," Jiang Qing said.

Kang Sheng said: "Wang Guangmei is an enemy agent and the case can be established. Write a report requesting her arrest as quickly as possible."

Xiao Meng told the court that he and his group thought that rather sudden and were very perturbed. They felt that much remained to be investigated and there was no solid evidence. This presented difficulties in drafting the report. However, the special group complied, not daring to disobey orders.

They worked through the night and arrived at this formulation: "We may conclude, in the main, that Wang Guangmei is an agent of the U.S." But even this wording did not satisfy Jiang Qing and Kang Sheng, when the report was submitted to them the next day.

Jiang Qing drew a large "X" through it, and wrote: "Poorly done. Return to special group."

When they got the report back, Xiao Meng said, the group realized that they had displeased Jiang Qing. So he took the report to Kang Sheng. After reading it, Kang Sheng said: "Your report is useless. You have not understood what Jiang Qing and I said. You have not presented the problem clearly." Then he added: "Don't bother about the report. I will write it myself."

Xiao Meng said that in the report written personally by Kang Sheng, Wang Guangmei was charged with not only being a "U.S. agent" but also a "Japanese agent" and a "Kuomintang agent." This report also bore Jiang Qing's signature, Xiao Meng testified.

"Later, I was expelled from the special group and imprisoned for five years," Xiao Meng told the court.

Questioned, Jiang Qing first claimed that she could not remember and that she had difficulty in speaking. Later, in face of the testimony of Xiao Meng and other evidence shown to the court, Jiang Qing conceded that it was her handwriting. "I recognize it," she admitted.

Extorting Confessions

Hao Miao, Liu Shaoqi's former cook, was also summoned to appear as a witness at the December 3 session. He testified that Jiang Qing and her followers branded him a Kuomintang agent suspect and kept him in jail for more than six years to wring material from him for use against Liu Shaoqi and his wife, Wang Guangmei.

At midnight June 8, 1967, Hao Miao recalled to the court, he was taken from his hostel and thrown into jail. Throughout the dozens of interrogations during his imprisonment he was ordered to reveal the "crimes" of Liu Shaoqi and Wang Guangmei. "They pressed me constantly. They also said that if I did a good job in exposing them, I would be released immediately."

Hao Miao told the court that he was also asked many times whether he had known Wang Guangmei before liberation in 1949 and what he had done on her behalf during that period. He was asked whether he knew that Wang Guangmei was an "enemy agent." He was forced to write out all the names of guests Liu Shaoqi had received during his inspection and work tours about the country and to write about Liu Shaoqi's personal habits.

They found all his replies unsatisfactory, Hao Miao said. "They tried to persuade me to admit that Liu Shaoqi had 'turned revisionist, corrupted by my good cooking!' They said I was so completely influenced by Liu Shaoqi that I was a 'loyalist.'"

"Later, they began to torment me by giving me less and less food until I was practically starving. I was given only two cups of water a day. Sometimes, I would plead for more, but in vain."

"They took delight in working out new ways to torture me. I was in jail like this for more than six years. I have a heart ailment now and high blood pressure, because of those years of mental and physical torture. Today, I cannot do a normal day's work."

Before Hao Miao was summoned to appear in court as a witness, the judge questioned Jiang Qing whether she had approved his arrest. Jiang Qing replied: "I don't remember."

A request for the arrest of Hao Miao "for investigation" was then shown to the court. It bore the word "approved" in Jiang Qing's writing. Confronted by this evidence, Jiang Qing admitted that it was written by her.

The court on that day also investigated charges that Jiang Qing had given her approval for the illegal detention of other innocent people, including Yang Yichen, Vice-Governor of Hebei Province, in her attempt to extort confessions against Liu Shaoqi and his wife.

People Tortured to Death

The prosecution charged during a court hearing on December 5 that Jiang Qing was chiefly responsible for the deaths of many innocent people tortured to extort "evidence" against Liu Shaoqi.

The First Tribunal saw through an epidiascope a report dated July 18, 1967, written by the "group for investigating into the special case of Liu Shaoqi and Wang Guangmei," on the detention and investigation of Yang Chengzuo, a professor of the China People's University in

Beijing, and his wife, Yuan Shaoying. A comment on the report in Jiang Qing's handwriting read, "approved."

Asked if the comment "approved" was written by her, Jiang Qing replied: "It is my handwriting, but I don't remember."

The court then summoned Zhou Yaocheng, a member of the special group, to appear as a witness. Zhou testified that the mission of the special group was to find material, through the investigation of Yang Chengzuo and his wife, to incriminate Wang Guangmei as a U.S. strategic intelligence service agent and so discredit and destroy her husband, Liu Shaoqi.

The witness said that at the time of Yang Chengzuo's detention he was ill, suffering from chronic hypertension, diabetes and arteriosclerosis. The special group suggested giving him a general health check and a cerebral angiography, but Jiang Qing objected. The witness added that Jiang Qing instructed the special group to "squeeze what we need out of Yang before he dies." When the victim's conditions became critical Jiang Qing also ordered the group "to quickly step up" the interrogations. The 65-year-old professor died as a result of this grilling. Before China's liberation in 1949, Yang was a professor of the Catholic University in Beijing, where Wang Guangmei had studied.

The court also took notice of the report submitted to Jiang Qing by the special group on "intensifying the interrogation of Zhang Zhongyi." Zhang was a professor of the Hebei Provincial Normal College in Beijing. Jiang Qing had circled her own name on the report marking her approval.

The prosecution pointed out that although Professor Zhang was once Acting Secretary-General of the Catholic University in pre-liberation Beijing, where Wang Guangmei studied, Zhang did not know Liu Shaoqi, nor did he know Wang. However, the court was told, Zhang was selected by the special group as a "key figure" for extorting confession because Zhang knew Professor Yang and his wife, both of whom knew Liu Shaoqi's wife.

In 1967, with Jiang Qing's permission, the prosecution told the court, the 67-year-old professor was unlawfully arrested, sequestered and interrogated. Zhang was a terminal liver cancer patient. Jiang Qing none the less approved and ordered "intensified interrogation." After his death, the special group wrote in a report:

"We organized a high-powered group for the interrogation and mounted successive political assaults. In the 27 days of his detention, we interrogated him 21 times, bringing increasing pressure to bear on him, and finally forced him to confess, bit by bit, material concerning Wang Guangmei as a special agent."

More than 80 tape recordings were made of the interrogations of Zhang Zhongyi, but only 20 were left, the court was told. When some of the remaining tapes were heard in court, the public were shocked and angered. They heard the weak cries of the old man being interrogated. They heard him gasping and struggling. They heard him being forcibly held down for administering medicine. They heard the threats and shouts of his interrogators and the feeble, confused protests and answers of the dying man.

The last interrogation of Zhang, on October 31, 1967, lasted 15 hours, the prosecution said. The old man died two hours later. According to the testimonies of those present at that last interrogation, the victim continued to deny that Wang Guangmei was an enemy agent. This was entered in the records taken verbatim during the interrogation. The following are some of the questions and answers from the last few pages of the records of the interrogation presented to the court:

Q: What espionage activities was Wang Guangmei engaged in?"

A: I hope to get this question clear.

Q: This is your chance. Do you want to take the question along into the coffin with you?

A: No. I am not clear at all about this question ... I cannot cook up a story, either.

Q: You are making yourself a nuisance. You are resisting to the end.

A: I've never thought about that.

Q: Why don't you confess? Do you want to put yourself against the people to the very end? Who is Wang Guangmei?

A: She is a Communist.

The tapes played back showed that Zhang's speech was slurred and quite confusing. In one recording, when forced to say what kind of person Wang Guangmei was, he first replied, "I cannot say clearly what kind of person she is." Further pressed, he said, "Wang Guangmei ... though a secret agent, is a very concrete enemy agent." And he added that he had learned this from "our government communique."

Doctors and other medical staff present during the interrogations of Professor Zhang also testified in court that during the period of his detention Zhang was suffering from severe cirrhosis of the liver, and that he had been interrogated even while in a coma and receiving intravenous glucose drips.

The third person who was imprisoned and tortured to death in connection with this charge was Wang Guang'en, a civilian of Tianjin, the prosecution said. When Liu Shaoqi was arrested in Shenyang in 1929, Wang Guang'en was an assistant manager of a cotton mill in Shenyang. A report on the detention of Wang Guang'en by the group handling Liu Shaoqi and Wang Guangmei's case, dated

July 19, 1967, was read in court and shown through the epidiascope. Jiang Qing circled her name on this report to indicate that she had read and approved it. Wang died under torture 40 days after his detention.

FALSE CHARGES AGAINST PREMIER ZHOU ENLAI*

After Liu Shaoqi was overthrown, the Gang of Four consisting of Jiang Qing, Zhang Chunqiao, Yao Wenyuan and Wang Hongwen, stepped up their efforts to frame Premier Zhou Enlai. Deng Xiaoping, who reappeared as a Party and state leader in 1973, was also made a main target of their attack.

According to the indictment, when preparations were being made in October 1974 for the convocation of the Fourth National People's Congress, Chairman Mao proposed that Deng be appointed the First Vice-Premier of the State Council. The Gang of Four saw this as a barrier to their usurping Party leadership and state power. At a secret meeting called by Jiang Qing on October 17, 1974, it was decided that Wang Hongwen should go to Changsha the following day to see Chairman Mao and make false charges against Zhou, Deng and other Party and state leaders. At that time, Chairman Mao was recuperating in Changsha and Premier Zhou was hospitalized in Beijing.

---

* Court investigation established that the charges made against the four accused in this respect did not fall within the scope of a criminal offence. Thus the issue of criminal liability on this question was not pursued in the verdict.

Following is a brief account of the investigation hearings held on November 24, 26 and 27 by the First Tribunal.

On November 24, Wang Hongwen and Yao Wenyuan were called before the First Tribunal. A deposition made by Zhang Yufeng, a staff member who was present during Wang Hongwen's conversation with Chairman Mao on October 18, 1974 in Changsha, was read out to the court. It quoted Wang as saying: "Although the Premier is ill and hospitalized, he is busy summoning people for talks far into the night. Almost every day someone goes to his place. Comrades Deng Xiaoping, Ye Jianying and Li Xiannian are frequent visitors," and "that these people come and go frequently at this time has something to do with appointments to be made at the Fourth National People's Congress."

When Wang Hongwen was asked if he had said this, Wang answered that he did say something to this effect, adding: "Those were Jiang Qing's remarks which I passed on," and "those remarks relating to nominations at the Fourth National People's Congress were Zhang Chunqiao's."

"Actually a Conspiratorial Activity"

When he was asked to give the reason for going to Changsha without the knowledge of Premier Zhou and other Members of the Political Bureau, Wang replied: "It was actually a conspiratorial activity, so Premier Zhou and the Political Bureau were not informed of it." Wang also told the court that his going to Changsha was "to prevent Deng Xiaoping from becoming First Vice-Premier."

Wang Hongwen admitted that he had said to Chairman

Mao that "the atmosphere in Beijing now is very much like that of the [1970] Lushan Meeting." He said that this expression actually came from Yao Wenyuan. It implied that Zhou Enlai, Deng Xiaoping and others were "colluding to usurp power" as Lin Biao had done during the 1970 Lushan Meeting.*

Zhang Yufeng's deposition also said: "Chairman Mao told Wang Hongwen that he should, after getting back, have more talks with the Premier and Comrade Ye Jianying and should not gang up with Jiang Qing, and that he should be wary of her."

Asked how he had carried out this instruction of Chairman Mao's, Wang Hongwen said that he "did nothing to implement it."

After Wang Hongwen was led away, Yao Wenyuan was led into the dock. Yao admitted that the trip to Changsha to make those reports to Chairman Mao was Jiang Qing's idea, and that "in fact, it was aimed at affecting the decision Chairman Mao had made," namely, to prevent Deng Xiaoping from becoming First Vice-Premier. He also admitted having said that "the atmosphere is like that of the Lushan Meeting." To other questions he either mumbled that he did not remember or answered, "I can't confirm or deny."

Jiang Qing was brought before the court on November 26 at a hearing to investigate into the charges concerning the Changsha incident.

---

* In late August 1970, at the Second Plenary Session of the Ninth Party Central Committee held at Lushan, Lin Biao led his accomplices to mount a sudden offensive at the meeting to have the agenda changed. Ignoring the original agenda, Lin Biao spoke first and advocated the necessity of retaining the post of State Chairman. (Chairman Mao had repeatedly suggested that in the forthcoming revision of the Constitution of the P.R.C., such a post should not be retained and that he would not accept it if it were.) Then members of the Lin Biao clique simultaneously launched "an offensive" in group discussions. Their aim was to make Lin Biao Chairman of the People's Republic.

To all the questions the judge asked her Jiang Qing replied, "I don't know" or "I don't know, either" or "How could I know what was said."

Testimonies Given by Two Witnesses

Later, Wang Hairong (then Vice-Minister of Foreign Affairs) and Tang Wensheng (an English interpreter for Chairman Mao) appeared in court as witnesses. Wang Hairong testified that on October 18, 1974, Jiang Qing twice summoned her and Tang to Diao Yu Tai, first during the day and then in the evening, asking them to take the opportunity of accompanying foreign guests to Changsha to make a "very important" report to Chairman Mao.

According to the two witnesses, Jiang told them in the morning meeting that she had had a row the previous night with Deng Xiaoping at a Political Bureau meeting over the question of the China-made freighter *Fengqing*. Deng Xiaoping had walked out immediately afterward, breaking up the meeting. Jiang Qing also said that the Premier was not really recuperating in the hospital, but was "colluding" with Deng Xiaoping and Ye Jianying and that the Premier was their behind-the-scene boss.

Jiang Qing summoned the two of them to Diao Yu Tai for the second time on the evening of the same day. They found Zhang, Yao and Wang already there with Jiang Qing. Zhang was asked by Jiang Qing to brief them on the general situation. All four asked Wang and Tang to report the situation to Chairman Mao.

"Considering that it was something serious, we hurried to the hospital the next day to report to Premier Zhou," Wang Hairong said. "The Premier said that he already knew what had happened at the Political Bureau meeting and things were not like what Jiang Qing had said. On the contrary, it was the four who had planned to attack Deng Xiaoping. They had done so many times before, and Deng Xiaoping had contained himself for a long time."

On October 20 after Chairman Mao's meeting with the foreign guests, Wang Hairong said, she and Tang Wensheng told him what Premier Zhou had said. Chairman Mao was very angry. He said that the freighter question was trivial and had already been settled. It was pointless for Jiang Qing to make such a scene. He instructed them to convey his words to the Premier and Wang Hongwen when they returned to Beijing. The Premier would remain Premier, said Chairman Mao. And preparations for the Fourth N.P.C. and personnel appointments should be handled by the Premier and Wang Hongwen together. Chairman Mao also suggested that Comrade Deng Xiaoping be appointed Vice-Chairman of the Party Central Committee's Military Commission and the Chief of the General Staff of the Chinese People's Liberation Army.

The testimony given by Tang Wensheng tallied with that of Wang Hairong.

On November 27, Zhang Chunqiao was asked three times by the court if he had colluded with Jiang Qing and others to make false charges against Zhou Enlai and Deng Xiaoping. Zhang refused to answer.

The court then played the recordings of the admissions of Wang Hongwen and of the account of the witness Wang Hairong, and had the written statements by Zhang Yufeng and Tang Wensheng read out.

Zhang Chunqiao sat mute throughout the session. The judge warned him: "Your refusal to answer questions does not affect the court proceedings. The court conducts the trial in accordance with the provisions of the Law of Criminal Procedure. . . . Article 35 of the Law stipulates that 'no accused shall be adjudged guilty and sentenced without evidence other than his confession; he shall be convicted and punished if there is sufficient evidence against him even without his confession.' "

MORE FRAME-UPS BY JIANG QING

On July 21, 1968, as Jiang Qing requested, Kang Sheng, a principal member of the Lin-Jiang counter-revolutionary cliques, prepared and provided her with a list of names of Members of the Eighth C.P.C. Central Committee. On this list, 88 of the 193 Members and Alternate Members were smeared as "enemy agents," "renegades," "elements with illicit foreign relations" or "opponents to the Party." Thirty other Members and Alternate Members were otherwise maligned.

Jiang Qing also directly framed and persecuted many other leading officials and prominent figures.

Following is a brief account of the court hearings held on December 12 and 23 to investigate these charges.

When asked if, at her request, Kang Sheng had sent her a top secret letter on July 21, 1968, with the names of the Central Committee Members whom they alleged to have committed "grave crimes" and why she had asked for such a list, Jiang Qing admitted that the list had been made up and sent to her at her request. She said she wanted the list because she was preparing the 12th Plenary Session of the Eighth Central Committee and the Ninth Party Congress which was to follow. She claimed that Premier Zhou Enlai had also given her a list, but without comments on the Members' political background. Kang Sheng had made those comments because he "knew their backgrounds."

The prosecutor pointed out to the court that Jiang Qing was trying to evade her responsibility by trying to mix up the two lists which were of quite a different nature. The prosecutor said that the list Jiang Qing had obtained from the late Premier in February 1969, was a copy of the official list distributed to all those participating in the preparations for the Ninth Party Congress. It was six months after Kang Sheng had drawn up the secret list, the prosecution stressed.

But Jiang Qing claimed that what she and Kang Sheng had done was "justifiable."

The prosecutor charged that "Jiang Qing and Kang Sheng cooked up the list for the sole purpose of persecuting those Party and state leaders and usurping Party leadership and state power." He told the court that he had evidence showing that Kang Sheng had personally defamed 592 people, including 120 Members and Alternate Members of the Central Committee, and that Jiang Qing had personally and publicly branded 172 people, including 28 Members and Alternate Members of the Central Committee. As a result of their unfounded accusations, large numbers of people had been cruelly persecuted, many of them maimed or killed and many of the victims' families broken up. In offering evidence, the prosecutor asked the court to hear some recordings of Jiang Qing's public speeches made between 1966 and July 1970.

Hurling Unsubstantiated Charges All Around

The judge then asked Jiang Qing if she had declared that Lu Dingyi (then an Alternate Member of the Party's Political Bureau and Head of the Party Central Committee's Propaganda Department) was "an agent of the Kuomintang secret service, the Bureau of Investigation and Statistics of the Military Council." Jiang Qing denied it.

A tape recording of Jiang Qing's talk to the representatives of the China Peking Opera Troupe and Central Philharmonic Symphony Orchestra on September 18, 1968, was then played in the court. Jiang Qing was clearly heard saying that Lu Dingyi was an agent of the aforementioned bureau of the Kuomintang. Questioned again, Jiang Qing admitted that it was "my voice."

When asked to substantiate her charge, Jiang Qing argued that "Lu Dingyi's brother was such an agent" and that he had "wormed his way into our army through the influence of Lu Dingyi." Challenged, Jiang Qing could not present any evidence to prove Lu's brother was ever a Kuomintang agent.

The court then read out the minutes of a January 3, 1971 speech of Jiang Qing's in which she alleged that Marshal Xu Xiangqian's wife, Huang Jie, as "a renegade," and that Marshal Nie Rongzhen's wife, Zhang Ruihua, was "an enemy agent." Jiang Qing in the speech said that after Chairman Mao Zedong, during the War of Liberation, had moved from Yan'an to Chennan village in Fuping County, Hebei Province, where the North China Command of the People's Liberation Army was stationed, the village was bombed by Kuomintang planes. She suspected the bombing was due to intelligence supplied by Zhang Ruihua to the enemy.

After hearing the recording of her allegations, Jiang Qing admitted that she had said such things. But, she claimed in defence that she had "heard it from Kang Sheng who had good reason for saying this."

The court then read out a statement entered as evidence by the Ministry of Public Security that the case involving the bombing had been thoroughly investigated not long after liberation and that the criminals had been found, arrested, tried and executed. Jiang Qing said: "Yes, they were all killed."

"Then why did you throw mud at Zhang Ruihua 20 years after the case had been settled?" the judge asked Jiang Qing. She had no answer.

"Jiang Qing smeared the two innocent women to get at the two old marshals," the prosecution pointed out to the court.

Exhibits were also placed before the court showing that Jiang Qing had falsely labelled Qi Yanming (former Vice-Minister of Culture) as an "active counter-revolutionary," Zhou Yang (then Deputy Head of the Party Central Committee's Propaganda Department) as a "special agent in the pay of the Japanese, U.S. and Kuomintang secret services," and Hu Qiaomu (former Deputy Secretary of the Party Central Committee's Secretariate) as a "turncoat." Listening to a tape recording of one of her public speeches in which these charges were made, Jiang Qing again admitted it was "my voice," but failed to answer when asked what grounds she had for making such accusations against these Party and government leaders. The judge pointed out that proclaiming these people to be "secret agents," "turncoats" or "active counter-revolutionaries" without any grounds whatsoever at a public meeting was a serious criminal offence and had, furthermore, led to the persecution of many innocent people.

Imprisonment and Torture

A tape recording played in the court proved that Jiang Qing, in a speech made on July 3, 1970, had vilified the then Acting Minister of Culture Xiao Wangdong as a "historical counter-revolutionary," and Wang Kunlun (former Vice-Mayor of Beijing), Qian Junrui (former Vice-Minister of Higher Education), Liao Mosha (a famous writer) and others as "proven vicious enemy agents."

The prosecution pointed out that as a result of these unfounded accusations by Jiang Qing, Qian Junrui and Liao Mosha were imprisoned for eight years, and Xiao Wangdong and Wang Kunlun, seven years. All of them were subjected to shocking mental and physical persecution.

Wang Kunlun who is at present Vice-Chairman of the National Committee of the Chinese People's Political Consultative Conference, appeared in court to testify. In the testimony, read out by his daughter Wang Jinling, he said: "I was branded an 'enemy agent' by Jiang Qing, Kang Sheng and Xie Fuzhi. . . . One word of theirs led to my arrest and seven-year imprisonment." He told the court that he was handcuffed and savagely beaten up in confinement and that he was now partially crippled as a result. Jiang Qing not only persecuted him but also charged that his wife, brothers, sisters and daughters were enemy agents too, and even his 15-year-old grand-daughter was implicated.

Liao Mosha, a famous writer, testified that he had joined the revolution when he was a lad. After stating that he had known Jiang Qing in 1933 in Shanghai, Liao declared: "She knows very well what sort of person I am. Yet she deliberately fabricated those charges against me."

When Liao Mosha was speaking of what Jiang Qing had done and of his own sufferings at her hands, Jiang Qing interrupted him time and again, screeching at the bench and abusing the witness. She defied warning and was removed from the courtroom upon orders by Vice-President of the Special Court and the presiding judge Zeng Hanzhou.

At the December 23 session President of the Special Court Jiang Hua warned Jiang Qing that she had laid herself open to the charge of contempt of court by her disrupting the previous hearing.

The Death of a Vice-Minister and a Model Worker

The prosecution charged that Jiang Qing framed and persecuted, among others, Zhang Linzhi, the late Minister of Coal Industry, Shi Chuanxiang, a national model worker (who is also dead), Ah Jia, former deputy director of the China Peking Opera Theatre, and Wang Kun, noted singer.

The depositions of a Vice-Minister of Coal Industry, a former student and a teacher of the Beijing Institute of Mining were read out in court, and a leading member of the ministry testified in court that the late Minister, Zhang Linzhi, was beaten to death at the instigation of Jiang Qing.

The testimonies said that on December 14, 1966, Jiang Qing accused Zhang Linzhi of being "a diehard member of the gang of Peng Zhen (victimized during the "cutural revolution," Peng was then Mayor of Beijing and is now Vice-Chairman of the Standing Committee of the National People's Congress). She incited the "rebels" of the Institute of Mining to detain, interrogate and torture the then Minister of Coal Industry.

Yang Ke, deputy secretary of the Party committee of the Ministry of Coal Industry, said in court that although the late Minister was sick, he was interrogated 52 times in 33 days and tortured to wring confessions out of him. Yang Ke said that, besides being beaten and kicked Zhang Linzhi was forced to wear a cast-iron headgear weighing 30 kilograms.

The witness said that on January 21, 1967, Zhang Linzhi was paraded at the institute campus and tortured until he died that night. Photos of Zhang Linzhi being publicly humiliated, the iron headgear he was forced to wear and the late Minister's corpse were shown through a projector. Yang Ke said postmortem revealed 30 wounds on Zhang Linzhi's body and a skull fracture.

In his deposition, Zhong Ziyun, Vice-Minister of Coal Industry, said that the late Premier Zhou Enlai had been terribly grieved by the news of Zhang Linzhi's death. "Depriving a person of his personal freedom and sequestration without trial are illegal," the Premier said. The Vice-Minister added that after the Minister was beaten to death, many other cadres of the Coal Industry Ministry were accused and hounded.

Witness Shi Chunli, son of the model worker Shi Chuanxiang, said that Jiang Qing was responsible for his father's death. He said his father, a night-soil collector in Beijing, had been honoured by the Communist Party for his long years of diligent work and had been received by the late Chairman Liu Shaoqi. A picture of his father shaking hands with Liu Shaoqi had been widely publicized in the newspapers. Jiang Qing labelled his father "a scab" for no other reason than to vilify the late Chairman. His father was made to parade through the streets with a heavy board hanging from his neck, and was beaten and tortured. He was not given food for many days, nor allowed to seek medical treatment. He died in 1975 after suffering great mental and physical cruelty at the hands of his persecutors. Shi Chunli asked the court to mete out severe punishment to Jiang Qing.

"You Have a Sordid Soul"

Ah Jia, former deputy director of the China Peking Opera Theatre, told the court how Jiang Qing had framed and persecuted him and his family and had hounded his wife to death. He said that in 1966 Jiang Qing had labelled him a "counter-revolutionary" out of personal spite and had told the "rebels" to give him the "full treatment."

Ah Jia, who was cruelly persecuted throughout the "cultural revolution," said: "She did this to me because I wrote the Peking opera *Red Lantern,* one of the eight 'model operas'. Jiang Qing claimed she had created."

He told the court that Jiang Qing had plagiarized his work, ransacked his house for his original scripts and wanted to seal his mouth. Eventually, he said, Jiang Qing sent men to his home to order him to deny he was in any way connected with the Peking opera *Red Lantern.*

Unable to control himself, Ah Jia turned to Jiang Qing and said: "You were once very high, but you are low and despicable. Your heart is vicious and your means are ruthless. You have a sordid soul."

He asked the court "not to show the slightest leniency towards this destroyer of China's culture and the murder of many thousands."

A recording of a speech made by Jiang Qing on July 3, 1970, accusing Ah Jia of being a "counter-revolutionary" was played in court. Again, Jiang Qing admitted that they were her words.

Recordings of other speeches by Jiang Qing played in court on December 23 included those in which she accused the singer Wang Kun of having "illicit relations with foreign countries," writer Liu Baiyu of being "a special agent," film critic Chen Huangmei of being a "traitor," and Sun Yang, former Vice-President of the People's University of China, of being an "enemy agent." All these spurious charges led to serious consequences. Sun Yang died in jail.

RANSACKING SHANGHAI ARTISTS' HOMES

In order to re-write her past as a film actress in Shanghai in the 1930s, Jiang Qing, together with Lin Biao's wife Ye Qun, instructed Wu Faxian (then Com-

mander of the P.L.A. Air Force) and Jiang Tengjiao (former Political Commissar of the Air Force of the P.L.A. Nanjing Units) to have the homes of five elderly Shanghai artists searched. The four men and one woman were abused and physically persecuted. Two of the victims died in their hands.

The victims were Zheng Junli (film director), Zhao Dan (film actor), Gu Eryi (film actor), Chen Liting (film director) and Tong Zhiling (Peking opera actress), all well-known figures. They had known Jiang Qing personally in the 1930s and were familiar with her past.

Following is a brief account of the December 9 court session investigating these charges.

During the hearing, Jiang Qing denied that she had anything to do with the search of the five artists' homes in October 1966.

Prosecution asked Jiang Tengjiao who was directly responsible for organizing and conducting the search to testify.

Jiang Tengjiao told the court that in early October, 1966, Wu Faxian summoned him to Beijing where Wu took him to see Lin Biao's wife Ye Qun. She asked him to find a certain letter written by Jiang Qing and told him to organize a search of the homes of five Shanghai artists and take all precautions to keep the action secret.

Masquerading As Red Guards

After returning to Shanghai, he first got the addresses of the five artists involved and, after repeatedly studying the job he had to do, worked out a plan of action. He organized some 40 young people and soldiers, who were to disguise themselves as "red guards" and search the homes of the five artists simultaneously in the early hours of October 9. These people were asked to seize all diaries, notebooks, letters, as well as all photos taken before the liberation and pictorials published before 1949.

The raids took place and the following day, Jiang Tengjiao said, he flew to Beijing with some of the items seized which he considered to be most important. He was received by Wu Faxian and Ye Qun, who heard his report in person and took away the material. The next day, Ye Qun telephoned Jiang Tengjiao, saying that "they have been submitted to the boss (Jiang Qing), who is very satisfied."

Shortly after Jiang Tengjiao returned to Shanghai, he was asked by Ye Qun to send the rest of the material to Beijing. At first she kept them in her own bedroom and later had them moved to the confidential files room of the Air Force Headquarters.

Then in January 1967, Jiang Qing asked Ye Qun to transfer the material to Lin Biao's official residence.

Zhao Gensheng, one-time clerical secretary in Lin Biao's office, testified in court that he was the person sent to fetch the material from the confidential files room of the Air Force Headquarters. He was told to leave the material in the kitchen catering to Lin Biao and his family. This he did.

As he was leaving, he saw Ye Qun and Xie Fuzhi (former Minister of Public Security and one of the 16 principal culprits, now dead) "burning the material obtained in Shanghai, with Jiang Qing watching a few steps away from the fire."

Testimony by Film Director's Wife

Huang Chen, wife of Zheng Junli, also gave testimony in court. She told the court how her home had been searched and how later, in 1967, her husband had been taken away to prison where he died without a trial.

"I didn't know that, Huang" Jiang Qing interrupted.

"Don't speak to me," Huang Chen said to the defendant sharply. "I know what you were like in the '30s. Wasn't your name Lan Ping then? Don't talk to me!"

Choking back her anger and grief, Huang Chen told the court how in June 1966, when the "cultural revolution" had just started, her husband was twice summoned to appear before Zhang Chunqiao, Jiang Qing's principal accomplice, and was told in no uncertain terms to hand over all the "relevant material" in his hands. Her husband had told her what Zhang Chunqiao had said: "Jiang Qing's position is different now. Some of her letters and other such things shouldn't be in your home. You'd better give them back to her." Her husband went carefully through his belongings, Huang said, and wrote to Jiang Qing saying that he had not kept those letters she wanted now, but had found a few old pictures from the '30s. The whole thing so worried and upset her husband that he said several times to her that every time he left home he wondered if it was for the last time.

Then in the early hours of October 9, a Sunday, a horde wearing red guard armbands broke into Zheng's home. They searched everyone in the house. They turned the house upside down and took anything that could be considered by the wildest stretch of imagination to be material they were looking for, even pieces of paper with hand-written characters. After this, the family was constantly harassed and abused. Then in 1967, Zheng Junli was forcibly taken away from his home and thrown into prison where he died.

Turning to face Jiang Qing, Huang Chen said in a voice charged with emotion: "You had my family broken up and my husband killed, just because we knew what you were like in the '30s, and because of that letter of yours, which you wanted destroyed."

Following this, the statement, written and submitted by the noted film actor Zhao Dan who died in October 1980, together with his wife, was read out in court. Their home had also been searched and they were imprisoned too. This statement corroborated the testimonies of the other witnesses.

Another witness, Liu Shiying, who directed one of the five groups carrying out the searches, testified in court that the searches were aimed at collecting all material connected with Jiang Qing and that Liu himself had personally handed over the looted material to Jiang Tengjiao.

Jiang Qing Directly Involved

To show that Jiang Qing was directly involved in the action, a statement given in testimony by a former Vice-Mayor of Shanghai, Liang Guobin, was read out. Liang testified that he was present on the first occasion when Zhang Chunqiao spoke with Zheng Junli and Zhang did ask the film director to hand over all the things that had anything to do with Jiang Qing.

A letter written by Zheng Junli to Jiang Qing in 1966 was shown to the court. The letter mentioned Zhang Chunqiao's talk about the letters and said: "I don't remember ever keeping those letters. . . . We never kept those letters of yours to us, nor those you wrote to Zhao Dan and his wife. Here are a few old pictures from the '30s. It's up to you to dispose of them."

Summoned to testify in court, Wu Faxian said that he acted in accordance with Ye Qun's instruction to give the assignment to Jiang Tengjiao. When Jiang Tengjiao came with the material obtained in the house-search, Wu Faxian said, he saw Ye Qun take it away, saying: "Give it to me. I'll take it to her. Jiang Qing is waiting for it."

Many More Victimized

In her attempt to do away with people who know her past, Jiang Qing persecuted far more people than the five artists. During the December 9 court hearing, Wu Faxian admitted some of the offences he had committed at Jiang Qing's instance:

(1) On the evening of February 22, 1968, Jiang Qing summoned him to Shanghai and instructed him to arrest leading cadres of the Shanghai Public Security Bureau — Liang Guobin, Huang Chibo, Wang Jian and some others, which he did.

(2) At a meeting in the Great Hall of the People in Beijing on the evening of February 23, 1968, Jiang Qing told him: "Sun Junqing* is a writer and deputy secretary of the Party Committee of the Shanghai Writers' Association. He has written a letter to me. Will you bring Sun to Beijing? I want to talk to him." Sun Junqing was taken to Beijing, framed and jailed.

(3) On the evening of March 2, 1968, Jiang Qing told Wu Faxian that a maid of her neighbour in Shanghai in the '30s "knew too much" about her. She said she wanted the maid brought from Shanghai to Beijing to meet her.

The maid by the name of Qin Guizhen was brought to Beijing, framed and jailed.

---

* In his capacity as deputy secretary of the Party Committee of the Shanghai Writers' Association, Sun Junqing once had access to some files of the 1930s and was thus suspected of being familiar with Jiang Qing's past.

INCITING VIOLENCE

An armed clash, called "the biggest riot in Shanghai," took place on August 4, 1967, after the Gang of Four had seized power in the city. On the pretext that a mass organization consisting of members of the Shanghai Diesel Engine Plant was "anti-Zhang Chunqiao and therefore a menace to the Shanghai Municipal Party Committee," Wang Hongwen incited some 100,000 people to surround and attack the plant. More than 600 persons of the plant were wounded, seized and tortured.

This came after another armed clash at Kangping Road in Shanghai. At least 91 persons were wounded in that incident, some crippled for life.

The Special Court docketed investigations of the two incidents as well as of the unlawful activities of a secret service group, code-named "244," personally directed by Zhang Chunqiao.

Following is a brief account of court sessions on December 4 and 6 investigating these charges against Zhang Chunqiao and Wang Hongwen.

At the December 6 hearing shots from a documentary taken of the armed clash in the Shanghai Diesel Engine Plant 13 years ago were shown. Wang Hongwen was seen interrogating "prisoners" and his followers beating these victims. Wang Hongwen himself had ordered the filming as a record of his "victory." Evidence was also exhibited before the court showing that as early as 1967 Zhang Chunqiao had acclaimed Wang Hongwen as "the leader of the Shanghai working class" and "our commanding officer."

Xu Panqing, deputy secretary of the Shanghai Diesel Engine Plant Party committee, testified in court that on August 4, 1967, Wang Hongwen organized over 100,000 people who arrived in over a thousand vehicles and boats to storm and seize the plant from the land and the water. The attackers charged into the plant, cut off water and power, and kidnapped, imprisoned and beat up over 600 members of the plant. "Among those wounded in the armed clash," Xu testified, "over 100 have been permanently crippled. Accountable material losses to the plant amounted to over 3.5 million yuan."

Confronted with the film and other evidence, Wang Hongwen admitted: "The armed clash caused several hundred casualties. . . . I plead guilty before the people of the whole country." He also admitted that he had directed the "Kangping Road incident."

The Kangping Road clash, according to testimony given by Zhang Chunqiao's wife, Li Wenjing, was engineered by Zhang Chunqiao from Beijing. Li's testimony, which was read out two days earlier, on December 4, when Zhang Chunqiao was brought before the court, stated that Zhang Chunqiao telephoned her on December 28, 1966 from Beijing asking her to tell Wang Hongwen and others to suppress the "Workers' Red Detachment," a mass organization in Shanghai. She promptly passed on this message to Wang and also to Xu Jingxian, another important member of the Shanghai gang. This led to the Kangping Road incident.

Xu Jingxian, summoned to give testimony, told the court that Zhang Chunqiao's instruction to suppress the Workers' Red Detachment were conveyed to him by Li Wenjing and he was told to pass them on to others.

Passages of Zhang Chunqiao's speech on March 8, 1967 to representatives from the city of Taiyuan, the provincial capital of Shanxi, were also read out in court. Speaking of the Kangping Road incident, Zhang had said: "We in Beijing were very worried to learn the news. . . . We telephoned the rebels and urged them to join the fight. The rebels waded in. . . . That trial of strength was a turning point. That battle paralysed the Shanghai Municipal Party Committee (the municipal Party committee before Zhang Chunqiao's take-over)."

Zhang Chunqiao refused to answer any of the questions raised by the judge.

Zhang and the "244 Group"

Then the court investigated the charge that Zhang Chunqiao had directed the "You Xuetao Group" (codenamed 244) to kidnap innocent people, search houses, secretly extort confessions by torture, collect and distort information and carry out other criminal activities.

The first evidence read out and shown through a projector was a one-year summary of its work by the "244 group," with remarks on the margin by Zhang Chunqiao and an attached letter addressed by You Xuetao (leader of the spy ring) to Zhang on November 30, 1968. According to the summary, between August 1967 and September 1968, the group provided Zhang Chunqiao with "investigation reports" and other papers running to some one million words. The summary showed that the group was engaged mainly in what it called "covert struggle."

A passage quoted from notes taken by You Xuetao on October 26, 1967, was also introduced as evidence. It reads: "Comrade (Zhang) Chunqiao instructed . . . be careful and cautious. There need not be too many people, but they must be absolutely reliable. Be careful. You can spy on others, but they can spy on you too."

A Shanghai actress, Zhuang Ruiyun, who had been a member of the "You Xuetao group," in a written testimony read out in court said that "everything the group did was top secret and nothing was allowed to leak out, not even its address or telephone number were known to any outsider." Their activities, she went on, included infiltrating organizations and winning people over. The methods they used, she confirmed, included "sex traps," "extortion of confessions" and "violence."

Wang Fang, the prosecutor, gave a brief account of how the "244 group" came into being. He said that You Xuetao was originally a sub-editor in a Shanghai newspaper. In the early stage of the "cultural revolution," he had formed a small band who called themselves the "Mine-sweepers." In early 1967 the "Mine-sweepers" spied on and secretly reported to Zhang Chunqiao activities within the Shanghai Garrison and about what certain people in Shanghai were saying about Zhang Chunqiao and his past. Zhang found the information gathered by these informers and stool-pigeons very useful and in April the same year, You Xuetao was appointed deputy chief of the mass movement section of the Shanghai Revolutionary Committee. This gave the ring, which was later expanded into the "244 group," a legitimate front for their clandestine activities. This group had its own special headquarters, special funds, cars, motorcycles, guns, special mini-recorders, etc.

It produced false charges against various leading cadres in east China and its activities were also directed at leaders in Beijing. Altogether the group concocted 26 cases involving 183 victims of whom five died.

Among the exhibits produced in court was the written testimony of He Xiuwen, former secretary of Zhang Chunqiao. He stated that, in October 1970, Zhang Chunqiao ordered him to burn large quantities of secret material collected by the secret organization.

Zhang Chunqiao later disbanded "244" because it was becoming too notorious to serve its purpose. However, its members still maintained contact with him and he shielded them. It was not until after the downfall of the Gang of Four that they were exposed.

COUNTER-REVOLUTIONARY PROPAGANDA

The political and economic situation in China began to improve in 1975 after thousands of veteran Party, government and army cadres, including Deng Xiaoping and others, who had been overthrown in the early period of the "cultural revolution," resumed work. The Gang of Four charged that this was a "Right deviationist wind to reverse the correct verdicts." In early 1976, Yao Wenyuan used the press under their control to publish a large number of demagogic articles accusing veteran Party, government and army cadres as being "bourgeois democrats," "old-line capitalist-roaders" and "turncoats." All these spurious charges had as their aim the re-overthrow of those veteran cadres and were an important link in the Gang's sustained effort to usurp supreme power.

In March and April 1976 Yao Wenyuan denounced as "counter-revolutionaries" the millions of people in Nanjing, Beijing and elsewhere who publicly mourned the death of Premier Zhou Enlai and condemned the Gang of Four. This propaganda directed against all upright Chinese people so infuriated the masses that it hastened the fall of the Gang in October that year.

Following is a brief account of the court sessions held on December 8 and 10 to investigate relevant charges against Yao Wenyuan.

Yao Wenyuan admitted at the December 8 hearing that he had been behind those demagogic articles published by the national press in early 1976. They were "directed at those veteran cadres who had resumed work for some time," he told the court. He admitted the revising and approving for release a number of defamatory articles which appeared in the *People's Daily* and the journal *Red Flag* (both organs of the Party Central Committee and therefore carrying great authority), which were under his direct control at the time.

Agitating Against Veteran Revolutionaries

Extracts from some of the articles revised and finalized by Yao Wenyuan were read out in court. An article signed by one of the "authoritative" writing groups* at that time, which was entitled "On 'Taking the Three Directives** as the Key Link' " and published in the *People's Daily* on February 29, 1976, alleged that veteran cadres were a "Right deviationist force for reversing the verdicts passed on them" a few years earlier. It claimed that "when the banner for 'taking the three directives as the key link' was raised, the Right deviationist forces for reversing verdicts quickly rallied under this revisionist flag and worked energetically for a capitalist restoration."

The *People's Daily* on March 3, 1976 carried an article calling veteran cadres "fanatics for capitalist restoration." These people were launching "counter-attacks to settle old scores," the article thundered.

In the No. 3 issue of *Red Flag* of the same year, a signed article put forward the formulation "from bourgeois democrats to capitalist-roaders" charging that veteran revolutionaries in the Party were now "capitalist-roaders" and were only "bourgeois democrats" when they joined the revolution.

---

* The Gang of Four had under them a number of writing groups whose job it was to turn out articles serving the interest of the Gang. Those "keynote" articles were either signed Chi Heng, Liang Xiao, Ren Ming, or Tang Xiaowen, etc.
** The three directives were "studying theory and combating and preventing revisionism; stability and unity; and pushing the national economy forward." The Gang of Four charged that Deng Xiaoping had formulated the slogan "Taking the three directives as the key link," and denounced it as a revisionist programme issued to divert the nation's attention away from the call "Taking class struggle as the key link."

Lin Zhaomu and Xu Jiansheng, responsible members of the editorial department of the journal *Red Flag* in 1976, testified in court that the abovesaid article denigrating veteran cadres and inciting people to overthrow them had been written on Yao Wenyuan's instructions. Yao himself had decided on the content and chosen the title of the *Red Flag* (No. 3) article which provided a "theoretical basis" for the attack on veteran cadres. During the writing, Yao had twice given verbal instructions, read the article five times and revised it three times.

In his testimony, Xu Jiansheng said that in a talk with the leading members of the editorial department of the journal on February 6, 1976, Yao Wenyuan charged that Deng Xiaoping was "negating the principle of three-in-one combination of old, middle-aged and young cadres"* when he proposed the reorganization of those inefficient ("weak, lazy and loosely knit" in Deng's words) leading bodies in the government and the People's Liberation Army. At Yao Wenyuan's instruction, an article on "three-in-one" was written and submitted to him for his approval. Revising the article, Yao commented on the margin of the manuscript: "His (Deng Xiaoping's) organizational line serving the revisionist political line must be criticized."

Libelling Millions of People

At the December 10 hearing, Yao Wenyuan admitted that he had labelled as "counter-revolutionaries" all those people who had mourned the death of Premier Zhou Enlai and condemned Zhang Chunqiao in early 1976.

---

* The principle of "three-in-one" trumpeted by the Gang of Four had as its ulterior motive to oust from office those veteran revolutionaries and intellectuals not to the liking of the Gang and its followers.

Prosecution's evidence adduced in court proved how Yao Wenyuan had verbally and in print attacked those who had laid wreaths in memory of Premier Zhou at Beijing's Tian An Men Square in April 1976. An estimated total of two million had gone to the square in the first few days of April to express their grief.

The manuscript of a report presented as evidence in court showed the phrase "this is aimed at overthrowing the socialist revolution" inserted in Yao's handwriting. Another manuscript showed he had added the sentence: "This is just the same as those seditious reactionary slogans in other places." Other evidence presented showed that Yao Wenyuan had denounced the big-character posters written by people in Nanjing denouncing Zhang Chunqiao as proof of a "counter-revolutionary adverse current."

The judge asked him: "When people in Nanjing put up big-character posters against Zhang Chunqiao, you called the action a 'counter-revolutionary adverse current.' But during the 'cultural revolution' this kind of posters was put up against almost every veteran revolutionary. Why didn't you call that a 'counter-revolutionary adverse current'? Why were you so 'sensitive' when Zhang Chunqiao was being denounced in posters?"

Yao Wenyuan stuttered and blinked but failed to give an answer.

Exhibits were also produced showing how Yao Wenyuan had tampered with news reports about the "Tian An Men event" in April 1976. He deleted references to people going to Tian An Men to mourn Premier Zhou and put in "counter-revolutionaries," "bad people," and "reactionary forces" to describe the mourners.

The court was shown an entry in Yao Wenyuan's diary dated April 3, 1976, which contained the following passage: "Why can't we have a batch of those counter-revolutionaries shot? Dictatorship is, after all, not embroidery-making."

Yao Wenyuan admitted writing it. But he argued: "Although I wrote about shooting people, it was only a fleeting thought." He also insisted that he had done all this in the historical circumstances of the time.

The court also investigated the charge that Yao Wenyuan was responsible for sending people to collect information maligning leading cadres at central and local levels.

Lu Ying, former editor-in-chief of the *People's Daily*, and Liu Zhiping, also a former leading member of the paper, were summoned to testify in court. They proved the charge.

———◆———

MASS PERSECUTION — SOME EXAMPLES

As a result of instigation and instructions from the Lin Biao and Jiang Qing cliques and their core elements, huge numbers of frame-ups were engineered everywhere throughout the country. Numerous Party, government and army cadres and other innocent people in all parts of China were falsely charged and persecuted.

The First Tribunal's investigation of charges against Chen Boda on November 29 pinpointed some shocking examples.

At a court hearing on November 29, Chen Boda admitted that he was responsible for that *People's Daily* (which, as the Party organ, had great authority) editorial "Sweep Away All Monsters and Demons."

Nationwide Chaos

The editorial in question was published on June 1, 1966. It implied that many leading cadres were "representatives of the bourgeoisie," noted intellectuals, specialists and scholars were "reactionary bourgeois scholars and authorities" and many prominent people in various walks of life were "monsters." "Knock them all down, humble them all," the editorial urged.

Large numbers of Party and government cadres and other innocent people were publicly abused and humiliated, and "swept out like rubbish." Many were thrown into prison or even killed. The country was thrown into chaos.

"The editorial was approved by me. I dictated the content and they took it down. Dictating it was equivalent to writing it myself," Chen Boda admitted.

Testimony given by the two writers who had drafted the editorial was read out in court. It said that on the morning of May 31, 1966, they were summoned by Chen Boda and Kang Sheng to Diao Yu Tai (the state guest house in Beijing) and were told by Chen Boda what to write for the editorial. As Chen Boda instructed, they worked up a draft of the editorial, giving it the title, "Advance from Strength to Strength and Carry the Great Proletarian Cultural Revolution Through to the End." Chen Boda twice revised the draft and changed the title to "Sweep Away All Monsters and Demons."

The second draft of the editorial, with the title and wording revised and finalized by Chen Boda and the revisions in his handwriting, was shown to the court through an epidiascope (see p. 8 of pictorial section). Chen admitted that the revisions were made by him and that he should bear all responsibility for the editorial.

2,955 People Hounded to Death

At the November 29 hearing, the First Tribunal also investigated into the facts surrounding the charge that Chen Boda trumped up the case of the eastern Hebei Party organization. The minutes of Chen's speech of December 26, 1967, a speech made in the mining town of Tangshan east of Beijing on the Party organization in eastern Hebei Province, were read out and a recording of the speech was played in court. Chen Boda said in this speech that the Party organization in eastern Hebei Province "was probably a party of Kuomintang-Communist co-operation and, in fact, it might be Kuomintang members and renegades who played the dominant role."

On his word and at his instigation, more than 84,000 Party cadres and ordinary people were persecuted and 2,955 of them died as a result.

"Did you have any grounds for making that charge against the Party organization in eastern Hebei Province?" the judge asked Chen Boda.

"None at all. I spoke without any foundation. I plead guilty," Chen Boda replied.

In his speech, Chen Boda also hurled false charges at Yang Yuan, then First Secretary of the Tangshan City Party Committee, and Bai Yun, the former Mayor of Tangshan and her husband, Zhang Da, then Party secretary at a state-owned orchard and others. As a result, certain people in Tangshan engineered the case of a so-called "Yang-Bai anti-Party group." A witch-hunt was unleashed to "pull up the roots of the Yang-Bai group" and to dig out its "social foundations."

The case of the "Yang-Bai group" ultimately implicated 1,604 cadres in 29 central departments and 24 provinces and municipalities, and 737 of them were branded as renegades, enemy agents, Kuomintang elements or capitalist-roaders. The charges, though unfounded, carried grave consequences to the victims.

In a written testimony by Yang Yuan read out in court, he described how he had been intensively interrogated for a dozen nights on end following Chen Boda's inflammatory speech. He was later dragged from one Party institution to another, from school to school, to all the factories and villages throughout Tangshan prefecture. He was reviled, abused, manhandled and made to stand bent down, with his arms pinned behind him, for hours on end. He was savagely beaten. Condemned as an "active counter-revolutionary" and a "die-hard capitalist-roader," he was expelled from the Party and made to do forced labour under surveillance. His home was searched and ransacked repeatedly and many of his relatives too were persecuted.

Chen Boda admitted that his speech had had serious consequences. But he claimed that he "was indeed ignorant" of the fact that so many people had been victimized because of his irresponsible charges. In the end, he said that his speech had "served a counter-revolutionary purpose."

On November 28, the court heard the charge that Chen Boda had made use of the case of the "Extraordinary Central Committee of the C.P.C." leaflet,* a case which had already been solved in Tianjin in November 1967, to frame and persecute Zhu De, Chen Yi, Li Fuchun and other Party and state leaders.

---

* In midnight of October 8, 1967, a worker from the city of Tianjin slipped a total of 80 leaflets into a number of postboxes in central Beijing. The leaflet was signed "The Extraordinary Central Committee of the Communist Party of China." The case was cleared up on November 20 of the same year when the man owned up, admitting that he had written, stencilled and mimeographed it by himself, "with no one else involved." Public security officers had verified the authenticity of the confession after thorough investigation.

The prosecution submitted in evidence to the court the minutes recording Chen Boda's meetings with Zhao Dengcheng, then a member of the leading group of the Ministry of Public Security, in April and August 1968. Chen suggested at the meeting that the "behind-the-scene bosses" still had to be tracked down. The prosecution charged that, on Chen Boda's instructions, Xie Fuzhi, then the Minister of Public Security, and Zhao Dengcheng fabricated the case of a bogus "Chinese Communist Party (Marxist-Leninist)," alleging veteran revolutionaries Zhu De to be its "secretary," Chen Yi the "deputy secretary and concurrently minister of defence," and Li Fuchun, the "premier." Its members were supposed to have included Dong Biwu (the late Acting Chairman of the People's Republic), Ye Jianying and other leaders. They were alleged to have had "illicit relations with foreign countries" and were attempting "to stage a coup."

Asked if he had any grounds for these allegations, Chen Boda replied that he suggested "tracking down the behind-the-scene bosses" without any foundation and was responsible for concocting the frame-up.

REBELLION PLOT IN SHANGHAI

Details of plans for an armed rebellion in Shanghai were made public before the First Tribunal on December 13 through documents, photos of weapons and transceivers, and testimonies given by followers of the Gang of Four.

According to evidence presented in court, in the ten days between September 18 and 27, 1976, after the death of Chairman Mao Zedong on September 9, Zhang Chunqiao met trusted members of the Gang from Shanghai three times and warned them that they in Shanghai must be prepared for "a grave test and for war."

On October 6, 1976, the Gang of Four was smashed, but the news was held back during the first few days. The Gang's confederates in Shanghai were tipped off by a phone call from agents they had planted in Beijing. According to their pre-arranged code, "Mother has a myocardial infarction," they learned that the worst had happened to their "seniors." They immediately went about deploying the militia for an armed rebellion.

Xu Jingxian and Wang Xiuzhen (both former secretaries of the Shanghai Municipal Party Committee of the C.P.C. and vice-chairmen of the Shanghai Municipal Revolutionary Committee) decided on setting up two secret operation command posts for the armed rebellion, and divided the militia into two commands: the first with Xu as its head was to take charge of the general situation and take over the newspaper offices and the radio station; the second with Wang Xiuzhen as its head was to take control of the city's trade unions, youth league, women's federation and public security, and would be directly in command of armed operations.

The municipal militia headquarters called up its forces, organized drivers and distributed ammunition. Groups of armed militiamen were deployed at strategically important points in the city proper and reinforcements were sent to guard the radio station and newspaper offices. Armed militiamen patrolled the city day and night.

Steps were taken to bring the city's administrative centre and main transport routes under their control. Three cordons were thrown up between the heart of Shanghai and its outskirts and pass words and codes were

*worked out. Fifteen transmitter-receivers were installed
and two communications networks formed.*

*But things did not go as the rebels anticipated. First,
the Party Central Committee was aware of the possibility
of armed rebellion and adopted resolute measures, including the summoning of Ma Tianshui, Xu Jingxian and
Wang Xiuzhen to Beijing, one after another, and sending
a group of experienced cadres to Shanghai; second, the
ground, air and navy units of the People's Liberation
Army had received orders and were ready to take action
at a moment's notice to put the rebellion down; and third,
the people of Shanghai would firmly resist any attempt
at rebellion. Even militiamen who had been hoodwinked,
soon turned around the muzzles of their guns when they
learned the truth. The armed rebellion plotted by Wang
Hongwen, Zhang Chunqiao and others collapsed.*

*Following is a brief account of the December 13 court
hearing on the attempted rebellion.*

Answering questions raised by the judge, Wang Hongwen admitted that the attempted armed rebellion in
Shanghai was the consequence of the Gang of Four
building up a factional armed force over a long period of
time and that he and Zhang Chunqiao should be held
responsible.

A Factional Force Disguised as Militia

Wang Hongwen said that as early as 1967, Zhang
Chunqiao had instructed his followers in Shanghai to
set up a general headquarters for the people's militia and
as the first step, to organize 100,000 armed militiamen.
Not long afterwards, without authorization Wang Hongwen ordered factories in the city to manufacture rifles

for the militia. He acquired by fraudulent means from the P.L.A. units large numbers of rocket-guns, howitzers, tanks and other heavy weapons not issued to the militia. He, Zhang Chunqiao and others had organized several hundred thousand armed militiamen in Shanghai by 1973.

In July and August, 1976, while Chairman Mao Zedong was seriously ill, Wang Hongwen had gone to Shanghai to instruct the hard-core members of his faction "to be prepared for guerrilla warfare." He had urged them to draw more weapons from their arsenals.

Confronted with testimonies and other evidence presented in court, Wang Hongwen admitted he had made the following statements prior to the attempted armed rebellion:

"What worries me most is that the army is not in our hands;"

"We must be on the alert against the revisionists taking power"; and

"We must be prepared for guerrilla warfare."

Questioned by a judge, Wang Hongwen explained that by "revisionists" he meant "veteran cadres overthrown during the 'cultural revolution'." Wang claimed that it was Zhang Chunqiao who had first put forward the idea of fighting a guerrilla war. "When the militia was first set up, he made it clear that its purpose was to serve class struggle and the struggle between the two political lines in the Party," Wang added. The judge then asked Wang: "Did you mean that if the revisionists, or in your words, the overthrown veteran cadres, came to power, you would start a guerrilla war?" Wang replied: "Exactly."

Co-conspirators Testify

The bench then summoned Wang Xiuzhen to testify in court. She told the court that the armed rebellion she,

Xu Jingxian and other followers of the Gang in Shanghai were about to start at the time of the Gang's ouster in October 1976 was the "inevitable result of the great pains taken by Zhang Chunqiao, Wang Hongwen and Yao Wenyuan to turn Shanghai into their stronghold." She said that on many occasions Wang Hongwen had told her that the army must not be allowed to take control of the militia in Shanghai. The militia had to be in the hands of the (Shanghai) municipal Party committee and that reliance should be put on this force in a future war. She added that on September 23, 1976, Wang Hongwen had telephoned her from Beijing, saying, "The struggle has not come to an end. You people should heighten your vigilance. The bourgeoisie inside the Party will never be reconciled to their defeat. There are always some people who would want to bring Deng Xiaoping forward." Wang Xiuzhen admitted in court that after the downfall of the Gang of Four, because of these instructions of Wang Hongwen's, they had thought that revisionists had seized power in the Party Central Committee and that the time for a "severe trial" had arrived. Consequently, they had plotted an armed rebellion in Shanghai.

After Wang Hongwen was removed from the court, Zhang Chunqiao was led to the dock. Zhang sat tight-lipped, refusing to answer all questions put to him as he had done at previous court sessions. Half a dozen depositions and other documentary evidence were produced in court and two witnesses were summoned to testify. It was demonstrated that Zhang Chunqiao had started as early as in 1967 to build the Gang's own armed force in Shanghai by disbanding the old militia and setting up a new one.

The prosecution pointed out that the law in China placed all armed forces, including the militia, under the leadership of the Party Central Committee and its Military Commission. Militia units everywhere should be under the leadership and guidance of the respective local

People's Liberation Army commands. But Zhang Chunqiao, Wang Hongwen and their followers in Shanghai had seized control of the local militia from the P.L.A. Shanghai garrison.

Zhang Chunqiao's Secret Directives

Testifying in court, Xu Jingxian said that Ding Sheng, former commander of the P.L.A. Nanjing Units, had gone to Shanghai one day in August to meet secretly with Ma Tianshui (former secretary of the Shanghai Municipal Party Committee), Wang Xiuzhen and Xu himself. Ding had said that the army units stationed along the Wuxi-Suzhou-Shanghai line would not listen to him and that they posed a serious threat to Shanghai. Ding Sheng had warned the three "to be prepared for any eventuality." Thereupon, Ma Tianshui had given orders to distribute to the Shanghai militia some 74,000 rifles, 300 pieces of artillery and 10 million rounds of ammunition.

Not long afterwards Zhang Chunqiao received Xu Jingxian alone in Beijing. After hearing Xu's report of Ding Sheng's secret meeting in Shanghai and the hurried distribution of weapons there, Zhang Chunqiao said: "Keep your eyes open for new trends in the class struggle."

After Chairman Mao died, Zhang Chunqiao had issued a series of directives of a counter-revolutionary nature from Beijing to Shanghai. On September 28, 1976, Zhang Chunqiao had sent Xiao Mu, Wang Hongwen's secretary, with this message to his cohorts in Shanghai: "You must frequently analyze the class situation and be aware that there will be twists and turns in the struggle. The bourgeoisie still retain some strength. The problem is who will get the upper hand." Zhang Chunqiao also warned Xu and others: "Shanghai would face a severe trial" and "be ready for a war." "On October 8 when we learned that the Gang of Four had been smashed," Xu Jingxian went on, "I thought that Zhang Chunqiao's dire prediction had become true and that the 'severe trial' had arrived. According to Zhang Chunqiao's September 28 directive 'be ready for a war,' I joined the plot for an armed rebellion in Shanghai."

As the court session of December 13 drew to an end, the prosecution declared that the court investigation had proved that Zhang Chunqiao and Wang Hongwen were guilty of building a private army and engineering an armed rebellion in Shanghai.

FRAMING SENIOR OFFICERS AND OTHER PEOPLE

Other chapters have described how the Lin-Jiang cliques worked together to remove senior Party and government leaders by every means, legal and illegal. The conspirators knew the importance of the gun in seizing power, so they went about methodically capturing control of the armed forces by framing ranking officers and removing them from their posts.

From December 3 through December 11, the Second Tribunal investigated the charges in the indictment against the Lin Biao clique for falsely accusing and destroying leading cadres of the Chinese People's Liberation Army. Among those falsely charged and persecuted were highly respected veterans like Zhu De, Ye Jianying, Peng Dehuai, He Long, and Luo Ruiqing. The witch-hunt Lin Biao and his co-conspirators whipped up created havoc

*in the Navy, the Air Force, the P.L.A. General Political
Department and the P.L.A. General Logistics Department.
Altogether 80,000 people were framed and persecuted in
the People's Liberation Army and 1,169 died as a result.*

*Below is a brief account of the court hearings on these
charges.*

Marshals Maligned, Peng Dehuai and He Long Hounded to Death

Zhu De, for all his distinguished service as Commander-
in-Chief in China's long years of revolutionary wars, was
not immune to the conspirators' attacks. Qiu Huizuo, a
principal defendant in the trial, answering questions during the court hearing on December 5, said: "I had made
those false charges against Marshal Zhu De because I
stuck close to Lin Biao. I plead guilty."

On December 1, 1968, at a Party meeting of the P.L.A.
General Logistics Department, of which Qiu was then
the director, Qiu openly accused Zhu De of "harbouring
wild ambitions and desiring to become the leader." After
the meeting Qiu had the text of his speech printed and
circulated in the General Logistics Department.

Qiu admitted during the same hearing that he did not
have any facts either to support his accusations against
Marshal Xu Xiangqian (now Minister of Defence). The
text of the June 1967 circular branding Xu as a "big
time bomb planted in our Party and army as well as a
typical careerist and conspirator" had been revised and
finalized by Qiu, and this was proved in court with
material evidence and testimony.

Peng Dehuai, Member of the Political Bureau of the
C.P.C. Central Committee, was one of those top military
leaders persecuted to death by the Lin-Jiang conspirators.

A written statement the prosecution read out showed that Huang Yongsheng, had approved on November 3, 1970 a report prepared by the "special group for
investigating into the case of Peng Dehuai." The report
accused Peng of "consistently opposing the Party and
Chairman Mao, maintaining illicit relations with foreign
countries, and committing countless other crimes." It
recommended that "Peng Dehuai be dismissed from all
posts inside and outside the Party, expelled from the
Party for good and sentenced to life imprisonment and
deprived of civil rights for life."

Huang Yongsheng admitted at the court hearing that
he had signed and approved the report, but said in defence
that he "signed approval to submitting the report to a
higher level; not to sentencing Peng Dehuai to life imprisonment."

Huang also denied that he had anything to do with the
proposal for punishment before the "special group" prepared the report. But the record of a telephone call made
by Huang's secretary on Huang's instruction on August
14, 1970 read out in court showed that the accused
had clearly instructed: "a proposal for handling the case
may be put forward . . . and penalties recommended."

Defendant Wu Faxian admitted at the court hearing on
December 6 that he had fabricated charges against Zhu
De with the motive of pushing Lin Biao into a more
prominent position. He also said that the charges against
him in the indictment concerning the framing of Marshal
He Long on Lin Biao's instruction were true. It was
in the summer of 1966 that Kang Sheng, one of the six
deceased principal defendants, first falsely charged
He Long and some others of "secretly deploying troops
to stage a February mutiny." Marshal He Long was
greatly humiliated in the following years and was
persecuted to death.

Another Target: Ye Jianying

During a session of the Second Tribunal on December 3, Huang Yongsheng was proved to have approved a report in June 1967, alleging that Ye Jianying, Vice-Chairman of the Military Commission of the C.P.C. Central Committee, had been taken prisoner by the enemy during the battle of Yunmenling in Jiangxi Province in 1934. The report was purportedly aimed at "rounding up renegades" and was submitted to Huang by a leading personnel in the Guangzhou Municipal Public Security Bureau. A "plan for investigation, No. 1" appended to the report had Ye Jianying as the target of investigation. (In those days of persecution mania whipped up by the Lin-Jiang cliques, any revolutionary who had been captured by the enemy was presupposed to have capitulated to the captors and become a "renegade.")

Huang Yongsheng admitted, upon questioning, that he "knew that he (Ye Jianying) had never been to Yunmenling." The enemy newspaper reports that Ye had been taken prisoner "were fabrications," Huang added.

When asked about the confessions extracted under duress charging Ye Jianying and several other high-ranking officers with holding "clandestine meetings" in 1968 to stage a coup, Huang tried to deny he had been connected. But records of Huang's instructions of April 6, 1968 to another officer revealed his complicity. The prosecutor then read out in court a report levelling the same false charges against Ye and other officers. The report also contained Huang's comments of approval in his handwriting.

Prior to this, Li Zuopeng had appeared in court on the same day. Li, together with two other former members of the Navy, Wang Hongkun and Zhang Xiuchuan, was charged with writing a letter to the Party Central Committee falsely accusing Ye Jianying of nine "crimes," including "working together with Liu Shaoqi, Deng Xiaoping and Tao Zhu to usurp the leadership of the army and to oppose the Party."

Questioned about the letter and what facts he had to base his charges, Li replied: "No facts. They were all false."

Chief of General Staff Victimized

"Hatching a big plot" against the Navy was the false charge levelled at Luo Ruiqing, late Chief of the General Staff of the P.L.A., by Lin Biao and his accomplices. After evidence was presented proving that Li Zuopeng and other co-defendants had made this charge, Li admitted on December 3 that he had taken part in the framing of Luo, and he had been praised by Lin Biao for this. "Li rendered meritorious service in opposing Luo Ruiqing," Lin Biao had said.

Li Zuopeng's charges were part of the plot to get rid of Luo by the Lin Biao clique. The court heard on December 5 how Huang Yongsheng had purposely delayed surgery Luo (under detention as a result of the frame-up) badly needed, so as to exert greater pressure on him during the period of uninterrupted interrogations.

The court also read out co-defendant Wu Faxian's confession and a letter written by Huang Yongsheng and Wu Faxian to Lin Biao's wife, Ye Qun. Wu's confession revealed that, instigated by Lin Biao and Ye Qun, Huang and he had approved the postponement of Luo Ruiqing's surgical operation. In the letter they labelled Luo as "a counter-revolutionary who had committed heinous crimes."

Disturbing the Political and Logistics Departments

On July 25, 1967, Lin Biao initiated a move to "smash the Palace of Hell," the General Political Department of the P.L.A. Evidence presented during the December 5 session of the Second Tribunal proved that Lin Biao had called for this attack.

Huang Yongsheng took up the cry and also publicly vilified the General Political Department as a "Palace of Hell" and charged that the department "has been recruiting renegades during the reign of several directors."

Qiu Huizuo joined in the attack. Qiu declared in public that the class struggle in the General Political Department "must be completely uncovered and things there turned upside down." He charged that the department was "not much different from the Kuomintang secret service." Under his instigation, 59 army cadres in that department were hounded and attacked.

On Lin Biao's instructions, Qiu Huizuo also created havoc in the General Logistics Department of the P.L.A. His unfounded accusation that there were officers who were "traitors," "alien-class elements" and "elements having illicit relations with foreign countries" in the department led to a large number of cadres being imprisoned and tortured. The widow of one victim described to the court on December 9 how Qiu Huizuo had hounded her husband Tang Ping to death. Her testimony was a terrible indictment of the ruthlessness and cruelty of the plotters in persecuting veteran armymen. "What she said is entirely true. ... I plead guilty," Qiu admitted.

At the December 10 hearing, further evidence was submitted to prove the charge that Qiu Huizuo and his followers had brutally persecuted all who dared to stand up to Lin Biao and Qiu himself. Of 462 victims directly attacked in the General Logistics Department of the

P.L.A., eight had died unnaturally. In the 113 cases fabricated by Qiu and his co-conspirators torture was widely used to extort confessions. Large numbers of people were imprisoned and their families, friends and associates were also harassed and made to suffer.

Numerous Victims in the Navy and Air Force

Another leading member of the Lin clique, Li Zuopeng was accused of framing and persecuting senior naval officers. At the hearing on December 4, Li Zuopeng was questioned about his part in the persecution in 1967 and 1968 on Lin Biao's instructions. Photo-copies of documents with Li's remarks penned in about selecting victims to be attacked were shown. The accused, however, declared that he had either "not completely agreed" to some of the names, or "agreed outwardly but disagreed inwardly." Li's defence was rejected by the prosecution, who pointed out: "The evidence submitted has shown that Li Zuopeng did not raise any objection at all to the list of names of those to be attacked. On the contrary, 120 people were framed and persecuted with Li Zuopeng's knowledge, approval and connivance."

Similarly, Wu Faxian was charged with framing and persecuting officers of the Air Force. Evidence was submitted and testimonies presented to the court, and according to Wu Faxian's confession on December 9, he had been behind the attacks against 174 senior members of the Air Force. Wu Faxian said: "Lin Biao told me on several occasions that we should make use of the 'cultural revolution' to 'overthrow a number of cadres, protect a number of cadres and win over a number of cadres.' 'Win over' I had understood to mean getting certain cadres over to my side by first striking and then stroking them. Ye Qun said to me once: 'You should strike down all those in the Air Force who are against you!' "

It was revealed at the December 8 hearing that Huang Yongsheng, colluding with Liu Xingyuan, then Political Commissar of the P.L.A. Guangzhou Units, had given his approval to investigate into the history of the underground Party organization in Guangdong Province. Huang's letter of September 12, 1967 to Jiang Qing and the notes he had written on the margin of a report handed in by the "special group for investigating into the case of Zeng Sheng" (Zeng was then a leading member of the Guangdong Party organization) was read out in court. Huang had proposed "examining" the pre-liberation underground Party organization in Guangdong. This led to the persecution of more than 7,000 people, of whom 85 died. Evidence presented before the court also showed that Jiang Qing had given an instruction on "finding out the real situation of the Guangdong underground Party organization."

In addition, from May 1967 to November 1970, Huang and his accomplice Liu Xingyuan concocted the case of a "counter-revolutionary clique" within the P.L.A. Guangzhou Units, which resulted in 700 P.L.A. cadres being cruelly persecuted. Wen Niansheng, Deputy Commander of the P.L.A. Guangzhou Units, was one of those persecuted to death.

———————◆———————

ATTEMPT TO ASSASSINATE CHAIRMAN MAO

Having eliminated Liu Shaoqi, the late Chairman of the People's Republic, Lin Biao wanted the post for himself.

At the Second Plenary Session of the Ninth Central Committee of the C.P.C. opened in Lushan on August 23, 1970, Lin Biao insisted on retaining the post of chairman of the People's Republic, although the Central Committee had already agreed to Chairman Mao's proposal made in March 1970 that the Constitution be revised to abolish the position of chairman as head of state.

Lin Biao's bid for a "peaceful transition" to supreme state power was frustrated at the Lushan meeting. He then proceeded to his second step — an armed coup.

Lin Biao turned his attention to the Air Force whose mobility attracted him. He sent his son, Lin Liguo, to the Air Force. At Lin Biao's bidding, Wu Faxian, then Commander of the Air Force, placed the entire Air Force under the command of Lin Liguo. Lin Liguo used the power of this office to organize a special detachment of sworn followers to serve Lin Biao's scheme. This detachment was later named "Joint Fleet" by Lin Liguo.

In February 1971, Lin Biao, his wife Ye Qun and Lin Liguo went to Suzhou where they worked out moves for a coup.

Lin Liguo called a secret meeting in Shanghai on March 21, 1971, at which a detailed plan for a coup d'etat was worked out. They code-named the operation Outline of "Project 571" (the pronunciation of "571" in Chinese is similar to that of "armed uprising").

On March 31, 1971, Lin Liguo summoned to Shanghai Jiang Tengjiao, Political Commissar of the Air Force of the P.L.A. Nanjing Units, to take part in another secret meeting. Together with three other members of the hardcore "Joint Fleet," they set up a "command unit" for implementing the plan of the armed coup.

As Lin Biao and company were stepping up preparations for their armed coup d'etat, Chairman Mao Zedong left Beijing for southern China in August 1971. He stopped over in Wuhan, Changsha and Nanchang, where he talked with local Party, government and army leaders, explaining to them the significance of the struggle at the Lushan meeting. He criticized Lin Biao, Huang Yongsheng (then Chief of P.L.A. General Staff), Wu Faxian (then Commander of the P.L.A. Air Force), Ye Qun, Li Zuopeng (then First Political Commissar of the P.L.A. Navy) and Qiu Huizuo (then Director of the P.L.A. General Logistics Department).

In Wuhan, Li Zuopeng received on September 6 a confidential report revealing the content of Chairman Mao's conversations with the leading personnel. Li Zuopeng returned to Beijing the same day and informed Huang Yongsheng and Qiu Huizuo separately. That very night Huang Yongsheng passed on the information by phone to Ye Qun who was then in Beidaihe, a famous summer resort, with Lin Biao.

The confidential information spurred Lin Biao's decision to assassinate Chairman Mao during his inspection tour. Chairman Mao was then in Hangzhou.

On September 8, Lin Biao wrote an order for the armed coup d'etat in red pencil on a sheet of white paper. Ye Qun prepared a sealed document addressed to Huang Yongsheng. The same evening, Lin Liguo returned to Beijing by plane with Lin Biao's written order and Ye Qun's confidential letter.

In Beijing, Lin Liguo worked out with his followers plans to assassinate Chairman Mao while he was in the south by attacking his special train with flame throwers or guns, dynamiting a railway bridge when the train passed over it, etc.

On the evening of September 10, Chairman Mao's train arrived in Shanghai from Hangzhou. Lin Liguo and his followers thought Chairman Mao would stay in Shanghai several days. However, they miscalculated. Upon his arrival in Shanghai, Chairman Mao stayed overnight on the train and left Shanghai by the same train the fol-

lowing day, returning to Beijing at dusk on September 12. The plotters had no time to put their plans into execution.

After their plot to assassinate Chairman Mao Zedong failed, Lin Biao and Ye Qun decided to flee south to Guangzhou, taking along Huang Yongsheng, Wu Faxian, Li Zuopeng and Qiu Huizuo, and set up another "party central committee" there.

But the guard unit stationed in Beidaihe heard about Lin Biao's plan to flee south. Premier Zhou Enlai was informed of this, and he immediately instructed the guard unit to keep the situation under observation.

Knowing that Premier Zhou was aware of what they were planning to do, Lin Biao had to change the original plan. He decided to fly north. His plane took off pellmell at 0:32 hours, September 13. At 2:30 hours, the special plane 256, a Trident with Lin Biao, his wife and son and a few others aboard, crashed near Undur Khan in Mongolia. None of them survived.

Reprinted from *Beijing Review*, No. 51, 1980

The Second Tribunal investigated charges concerning the coup in six sessions from November 23 to November 29. Following are highlights.

On November 23, Wu Faxian admitted in court that he had recommended Lin Biao's son Lin Liguo for admission into the Party to show that he (Wu Faxian) had thrown in his lot with Lin Biao and was currying his favour. Later, on the instructions of Lin Biao and Ye Qun, he made Lin Liguo deputy director of the General Office and concurrently deputy chief of the Operations Department of the Air Force Headquarters.

Lin Biao's Son Put in Charge of Air Force

Wu Faxian also admitted that he had ordered without authorization that "everything concerning the Air Force was to be reported to Lin Liguo and everything of the Air Force should be put at his disposal and under his command."

At this point, the minutes of a working session of the standing committee of the Air Force Party Committee held on July 6, 1970 were read to the court and a slide of the document projected. These, plus testimonies by some former Air Force officers, corroborated Wu's admissions.

A photo of Lin Biao meeting with two principal members of the "Joint Fleet," Zhou Yuchi and Wang Fei, was shown. It was on that occasion that Lin Biao "suggested" that Lin Liguo be made the head of their "Joint Fleet."

A deposition by Liu Shiying, former deputy director of the general office of the Air Force Headquarters, was read out. The deposition said that the "Joint Fleet" was formed by expanding an investigation group headed by Lin Liguo with the approval of Wu Faxian.

Cheng Hongzhen, a former clerical secretary in the general office of the Air Force Headquarters, appeared in court as a witness. He testified to the division of work among the members of the "Joint Fleet," their clandestine meeting places and their counter-revolutionary activities.

The code names of the members of the "Joint Fleet," written in Ye Qun's own handwriting, were projected on a screen in the courtroom.

After these items of evidence were shown, Wu Faxian said: "My decision to put everything at Lin Liguo's disposal and under his command had a direct connection with these serious consequences. I was directly responsible for them."

Outline of "Project 571"

March 1971 saw the conspirators busily plotting an armed coup d'etat. Lin Liguo actively carried out the instructions of his parents.

Jiang Tengjiao, one of the principal accused, admitted to the court on November 25 that he took part in a secret meeting called by Lin Liguo in Shanghai on March 31, 1971 for the armed coup they designated *Outline of "Project 571."*

During the meeting which lasted the whole night, a "command unit" was established with Wang Weiguo (then Political Commissar of P.L.A. Unit 7341) made "head" in Shanghai, Chen Liyun (then Political Commissar of P.L.A. Unit 7350) in Hangzhou, and Zhou Jianping (Deputy Commander of the P.L.A. Nanjing Units) in Nanjing. Jiang Tengjiao was made "responsible for liaison between the three places to co-ordinate and concert action."

The court read out a deposition made on July 14, 1980 by Chen Liyun, the "Joint Fleet" member in charge of Hangzhou. The deposition, other documentary evidence and testimony tallied with what Jiang told the court. Zhou Jianping, the "Fleet" member assigned to the plotted coup in Nanjing, was summoned to the court to give evidence. His admission accorded with findings in earlier hearings.

Li Weixin,* who took a direct part in drafting the *Outline of "Project 571"* and who also attempted to flee the country after their plot fizzled out, was brought into court to testify. Li said that on March 21, 1971, in Shanghai, he had heard the conversation between Lin Liguo and two other "Joint Fleet" members, Zhou Yuchi and Yu Xinye. Lin Liguo had said that there was the likelihood of Lin Biao being kicked out of power at any moment. Therefore, they must up-schedule their plan to seize power. "A coup d'etat must be staged and full preparations made for an armed uprising," Lin Liguo had said. He had also said: "In view of the present situation, the Chief (Lin Biao) has asked us to work out a plan first. I have discussed it with him. . . ."

The court was shown slides of the draft for the *Outline of "Project 571"* (see p. 11 of pictorial section) with nine headings, such as: possibilities, basic conditions, policies and tactics, security and discipline, etc. This incriminating evidence was seized in a search of Lin Liguo's secret centre in the Air Force Academy of the P.L.A. after the conspirators fled.

---

* On September 13, 1971, soon after Lin Biao fled the country, Li Weixin and two other "Fleet" members, Zhou Yuchi and Yu Xinye, also tried to flee, but their helicopter was forced down. They decided to kill themselves. Zhou and Yu shot themselves dead, but Li only fired into the air, and was later taken alive.

Assassination Plans

On August 14, 1971, Chairman Mao left Beijing by special train for an inspection tour of southern parts of China. In the course of his tour he spoke with a number of local Party, government and army leaders, criticizing Lin Biao and his accomplices for their surprise bid at Lushan in August 1970 to retain the post of State Chairman, which Lin Biao hoped to take.

On November 25, Li Zuopeng admitted in court that after he had learned through one of his men the content of Chairman Mao's confidential talks, he immediately informed Huang Yongsheng and Qiu Huizuo of what he had learned.

Questioned by the Tribunal, Huang Yongsheng confessed that on the evening of September 6, 1971, as soon as he heard from Li Zuopeng the talks of Chairman Mao, he made a secret report to Ye Qun who was then in the summer resort of Beidaihe.

The logs of phone calls were exhibited. Entries in the logs showed that on the evening of September 6, Huang called Ye Qun up three times within 27 minutes. The first two calls found Ye Qun absent, but the third time they made contact and talked for 58 minutes.

Asked what was said over the phone and what followed, Huang replied that he had told Ye Qun everything Li Zuopeng had divulged to him.

Two days later, on September 8, Lin Biao issued a handwritten order for an armed counter-revolutionary coup d'etat (see p. 9 in pictorial section). The order, exhibited in court, read: "Expect you to act according to the order transmitted by Comrades Liguo and Yuchi." This incriminating evidence was found in the helicopter which also attempted to flee north soon after Lin Biao's defection but was forced to land.

This was corroborated by Jiang Tengjiao on his November 26 appearance before the court. Replying to the judge's questions about the plot, Jiang said that on the evening of September 8, 1971, in Beijing, Lin Liguo had shown him Lin Biao's handwritten order for the projected coup. "Having been assigned to Shanghai with the title of frontline commander," said Jiang, "I was to direct the operation to assassinate Chairman Mao."

Jiang also told the court: "We discussed three plans: one, attack Chairman Mao's train with flame throwers and 40-mm. rocket guns; two, attack Chairman Mao's train with 100-mm. re-assembled anti-aircraft guns at point-blank range; three, have Wang Weiguo shoot Chairman Mao with a pistol when he was received by the Chairman on board the train."

Jiang also disclosed that Lin Liguo, he and others had held four secret meetings in three days on September 8, 9 and 11 in Beijing to work out more details of the assassination. They discussed dynamiting the Shuofang railway bridge near Suzhou, bombing the train from the air, or blowing up the oil depot in Shanghai's Hongqiao airport when the train drew in and then assassinate Chairman Mao in the ensuing commotion. Jiang said that he had drawn a map during one of their meetings marking out the oil depot and the place where the special train would make a halt.

Depositions made by three accomplices, Li Weixin, Wang Fei (then deputy chief-of-staff of the Air Force Headquarters) and Guan Guanglie (then Political Commissar of the P.L.A. Unit 0190), testified to the holding of the four secret meetings and the content of their discussions. Hu Ping (then deputy chief-of-staff of the Air Force Headquarters) and Lu Min (then chief of the Operations Department of the Air Force Headquarters), who were two other accomplices in the case, gave parole evidence in court corroborating the facts.

However, after his arrival in Shanghai, Chairman Mao spent the night on board the train and left the next day — earlier than the conspirators had anticipated. The assassination plot fell through.

Huang Yongsheng was brought before the court on November 28.

Huang admitted he had been "a member of the Lin Biao counter-revolutionary clique," but insisted that he "had no special relationship with Lin Biao."

The defendant's assertion was contradicted by evidence and testimony submitted by the prosecution.

A written testimony from Wang Fei read out in court stated that on the very day Lin Biao issued his written order for the coup, Lin Liguo brought to Huang Yongsheng a sealed document from Ye Qun in Beidaihe to be delivered through Wang Fei. Wang Fei quoted Lin Liguo as saying: "When it (the coup) starts, your orders will come directly from Chief of the General Staff Huang (Yongsheng)." On September 9, Wang Fei said, Lin Liguo gave him a letter from Lin Biao addressed to Huang, to be forwarded to Huang "when necessary."

This "when necessary" letter was shown to the court through an epidiascope. It read: "Comrade (Huang) Yongsheng, I miss you very much and I hope you will be optimistic at all times. Take care of your health. If you have any problems, consult Comrade Wang Fei directly." The words "If you have any problems" in the letter were in reference to the imminent counter-revolutionary coup d'etat, the prosecution clarified.

Testimony given by six telephone operators read out in court showed that during the seven days following Huang's secret report to Ye Qun on September 6, 1971, Huang and Ye Qun spoke to each other 16 times over the telephone. The longest call made on September 10 lasted 135 minutes.

Later, Huang's former bodyguard, former orderly and former secretary testified in court that Huang Yongsheng had destroyed incriminating evidence after Lin Biao's plane crash on September 13, 1971.

The Lins' Escape

At the November 28 session, the defendant Li Zuopeng was questioned about the part he played in Lin Biao's escape after the plot to kill Chairman Mao fell through. Lin Biao and his principal accomplices had made hurried preparations to fly south to set up another "party central committee" and "government" to split the nation. A special plane, the Trident No. 256, in a nearby airport controlled by the Navy, was to be used to fly Lin south. As soon as Premier Zhou Enlai heard reports of Lin's movements, he immediately instructed Li Zuopeng not to permit the Trident to take off without a joint order from all four persons, namely, Zhou Enlai, Huang Yongsheng, Wu Faxian and Li Zuopeng.

When asked why in relaying Premier Zhou's order to those in charge of the airport he tampered it into "the plane must not be allowed to take off unless one of the four above-mentioned leading officials gives the order," Li Zuopeng could not explain. An officer in charge of the airport at the time testified in court that although Li Zuopeng had been told three times that very night that Trident 256 was about to take off, Li did not take any step to prevent the plane leaving.

In the afternoon of November 29, Wu Faxian was questioned on his role in connection with the defection of Lin Biao. The court heard that after Lin Biao's departure at 00:32 hours on September 13, 1971, Premier Zhou, at a little after 01:00 hours, ordered Wu Faxian to ground all planes throughout China. Nevertheless, more than an hour after the order was given, Zhou Yuchi, Yu Xinye and Li Weixin, all Lin Biao's sworn followers, still managed to get a helicopter into the air and tried to fly out of the country.

After evidence was introduced and the written testimony of Li Weixin read out in court describing how he and others had got the helicopter, Wu Faxian admitted that he had done nothing to stop the aircraft taking off.

On the same day, Qiu Huizuo made his appearance in the tribunal, charged with destroying evidence after Lin Biao's defection, including correspondence between himself and Lin Biao and Ye Qun, photographs, notebooks and other materials. Qiu admitted to the charge.

COURT DEBATE

The People's Court conducts all trials publicly, unless otherwise provided for by the present Law. The accused has the right of defence, and the People's Court has the obligation to guarantee defence for him.

Article 8 of the *Law of Criminal Procedure*

Upon completion of investigation by the Bench, the public prosecutor and the injured party shall have their say, then the accused shall make a statement in his own defence and the advocate shall offer a defence for him, and they may debate with each other. After the presiding judge declares the conclusion of the debate, the accused has the right to present the final statement.

Article 118 of the *Law of Criminal Procedure*

JIANG QING: "WITHOUT LAW, WITHOUT HEAVEN"

The Special Court held two sessions to debate charges against Jiang Qing on December 24 and 29. Jiang Qing refused to admit her guilt throughout the trial. She went so far as to declare at one court hearing that "I am without law and without heaven." The debate ended with the prosecution demanding that Jiang Qing be punished according to Article 103* of the Criminal Law.

* This article says: "Whoever commits any of the counter-revolutionary offences specified in this chapter (Chapter One: Counter-revolutionary Offences), with the exception of Articles 98, 99 and 102, and causes particularly grave harm to the state and the people in a particularly flagrant case may be sentenced to death."

Jiang Qing chose to defend herself instead of entrusting lawyers with her defence and spoke for nearly two hours on her own behalf. Unable to rebut the overwhelming evidence adduced by the prosecution, she shrugged off the charges against her as "negligible issues aimed at defaming me," an attempt "to pick a bone out of an egg."

Shifting Responsibility onto Chairman Mao

She argued that she had done everything during the "cultural revolution" "on behalf of Chairman Mao Zedong" or "according to his instructions." Again and again she repeated these assertions of hers: "Arresting me and bringing me to trial is a defamation of Chairman Mao Zedong," "Defaming Chairman Mao Zedong through defaming me," "I have implemented and defended Chairman Mao's proletarian revolutionary line." She shrilled: "During the war I was the only woman comrade who stayed beside Chairman Mao at the front; where were you *hiding yourselves* then?" — a statement that made it difficult for those in the public gallery to suppress their laughter — generals who fought hundreds of battles, pioneers in establishing revolutionary bases, underground workers operating at all hazards in the KMT-controlled or Japanese-occupied areas.

Jiang Qing declared: "Trying me amounts to smearing hundreds of millions of people." It "amounts to denigrating the proletarian cultural revolution in which hundreds of millions took part." It amounts to "preventing the red guards and little red guards in the cultural revolution from holding up their heads." She shrieked: "Now I'm doing my best for the defence of the proletarian cultural revolution." She attacked the redressing of wrongs done to innocent people after the fall of the Gang of Four as "actually a reversal of the correct verdict passed on them."

She shouted at the bench: "Like a monk under an umbrella, I am without law and without heaven." ("*he shang da san, wu fa wu tian*"; Since the Buddhist monk is bald and, being under an umbrella, can't see the sky, he is "hairless and skyless," a pun meaning "without law and without heaven." — *Ed.*)

Prosecution Refutes Jiang Qing

Refuting Jiang Qing's allegations, the prosecutor Jiang Wen said that during the "cultural revolution," Jiang Qing took advantage of various opportunities to frame large numbers of Party, government and army cadres and civilians, smeared people with such fabricated labels as "renegade," "enemy agent" and counter-revolutionary," detained innocent persons at will, rigged up false evidence, and concocted cases.

Jiang Qing colluded with Kang Sheng and Xie Fuzhi, he said, in directing groups of investigators to extort confessions by torture, and personally ordered "intensified interrogation" of Yang Chengzuo and Zhang Zhongyi, two professors who were in poor health and who succumbed to their torment.

Together with Kang Sheng and Chen Boda, the prosecutor said, Jiang Qing made the illegal decision to have the State Chairman, the General Secretary of the Party Central Committee and certain Vice-Premiers of the State Council framed, discredited and persecuted.

In July of 1968 Jiang Qing, with the aim of framing and persecuting Members of the Eighth C.P.C. Central Committee, asked Kang Sheng to hand over to her a list of the Committee Members. On this list, 88 Members and Alternate Members were labelled as "enemy agents," "renegades," "elements having illicit relations with foreign countries" or "anti-Party elements," the prosecutor said.

On March 2, 1976 Jiang Qing summoned leading members from 12 provinces and autonomous regions to a meeting at which she maligned Deng Xiaoping, calling him a "big quisling," a "fascist" and a "counter-revolutionary double-dealer."

It was about that time, the prosecutor said, that Chairman Mao denounced Jiang Qing for "interfering too much when she addressed a 12-province meeting, a meeting she called without any authorization."

Jiang Qing framed Zhang Linzhi, Alternate Member of the C.P.C. Central Committee and Minister of Coal Industry, as a "sworn follower of Peng Zhen" (Mayor of Beijing, also framed by the Gang) and incited persons ignorant of the facts to persecute him to death.

She framed Zhou Yang, Alternate Member of the C.P.C. Central Committee, as "renegade," "hidden traitor," "Kuomintang agent" and "Japanese agent."

Jiang Qing framed Shi Chuanxiang, a sanitation worker who was a national model, as a "bought-over scab," and she had him persecuted to death.

The prosecutor asked Jiang Qing whether Chairman Mao Zedong had told her to do all these things.

Jiang Qing framed and persecuted countless people, then attempted to place the blame on Chairman Mao so as to evade her responsibility and escape due punishment by law. This was unacceptable, said the prosecutor Jiang Wen.

Jiang Qing, the prosecutor recalled, had said: "Arresting me and bringing me to trial is a defamation of Chairman Mao Zedong." The prosecutor replied: "This is a vicious slander and vilification of Chairman Mao Zedong."

Chairman Mao's Contributions and Mistakes

Jiang Wen went on: "The people of all nationalities throughout the country are very clear that Chairman Mao was responsible, so far as his leadership was concerned, for their plight during the 'cultural revolution' and he was also responsible for failing to see through the Lin Biao and Jiang Qing counter-revolutionary cliques.

"However, the Party, the army and the people of all our nationalities will never, for this reason, forget or nullify Chairman Mao's great contributions to overthrowing the 'three great mountains' (i.e. imperialism, feudalism and bureaucrat-capitalism), founding the People's Republic of China and pioneering the socialist cause in China. Neither will they fail to sum up the experience and lessons of the ten years of the 'cultural revolution.' Our Party and state leaders have time and again declared that throughout his political life, Chairman Mao's achievements were primary, while his mistakes were secondary.

"These facts cannot be disproved and nullified by Jiang Qing, Lin Biao and company. It is futile for Jiang Qing to attempt to hide her counter-revolutionary crimes behind Chairman Mao's prestige."

Jiang Qing Rebutted by Chairman Mao

Jiang Wen said that as a matter of fact, Chairman Mao had repeatedly exposed and refuted Jiang Qing.

Jiang Wen specified: "On July 17, 1974, Chairman Mao Zedong said at a meeting of the Political Bureau of the C.P.C. Central Committee: 'She (Jiang Qing) does not speak for me, she speaks only for herself.' 'In a word, she represents herself.' "

On December 23, 1974, the prosecutor recalled, Chairman Mao sternly directed, "Jiang Qing: one, don't flaunt yourself in public; two, don't write instructions on documents irresponsibly; three, don't take part in forming a government." He also said on another occasion: "Do you think Jiang Qing has wild ambitions? In my view she has."

Jiang Wen then quoted Chairman Mao as saying towards the end of 1974 that "Jiang Qing has wild ambitions. She actually wants Wang Hongwen to be Chairman of the Standing Committee of the National People's Congress and herself to be Party Chairman."

At the beginning of 1975, Chairman Mao Zedong said: "After I die, she (Jiang Qing) will make trouble."

The prosecutor said: "These remarks by Chairman Mao Zedong made things very clear. Now, Jiang Qing still tries to describe her counter-revolutionary crimes as being carried out on behalf of Chairman Mao or in accordance with his instructions. Such lies can deceive nobody!"

Refuting Jiang Qing's allegation that "trying me amounts to smearing hundreds of millions of people," the prosecutor said: "This is a brazen insult to the people." He recalled the mammoth demonstration of Tian An Men Square on April 5, 1976 honouring the memory of Premier Zhou Enlai and condemning the Gang of Four, and the people's jubilation over the fall of the Gang in October of the same year.

"Jiang Qing represented none other than a handful of schemers, careerists, counter-revolutionaries, criminals, hoodlums and other dregs of society," Jiang Wen said.

Commenting on Jiang Qing's assertion that trying her would mean putting pressure on the red guards and little red guards of the "cultural revolution," the prosecutor said that Jiang Qing's counter-revolutionary offences had nothing to do with them. Those young people who were misled and corrupted by the Gang of Four, Jiang Wen said, "like the rest of the people, demand that you be brought to book for your crimes."

Lin-Jiang Collusion

Citing facts showing the collusion between the Lin Biao and Jiang Qing cliques, the prosecutor nailed Jiang Qing's lie that she was a "heroine" fighting against Lin Biao.

Before the Lin Biao clique was exposed and smashed in September of 1971, Jiang Wen said, the two cliques collaborated both openly and undercover in framing and persecuting Party and state leaders, suppressing cadres and the masses in an attempt to subvert the government.

The charges enumerated by the prosecutor included the framing and persecution of Liu Shaoqi, the State Chairman, and He Long, Luo Ruiqing and Lu Dingyi, all Vice-Premiers.

"Are these facts still insufficient to show that the Gang of Four headed by Jiang Qing and the group under Lin Biao were colluding counter-revolutionary cliques?" the prosecutor asked.

After the downfall of the Lin Biao clique, the prosecutor said, Jiang Qing gathered together its remnants including Ding Sheng, then Commander of the P.L.A. Nanjing Units, and Wang Huaixiang, at that time Political Commissar of the Jilin Provincial Military Area, for further counter-revolutionary activities.

"All this shows that the Lin Biao and Jiang Qing counter-revolutionary cliques colluded in usurping power while fighting over the spoils."

Abusing the Bench and Prosecution

Jiang Qing refused to reply to the charges against her as listed in the indictment, but dismissed them as "negligible issues aimed at defaming me." At the same time, she continued to attack the current Party and state leaders as "reactionaries," "counter-revolutionaries" and "fascists," and to hurl abuses at the bench and the prosecution. She did this once again when she was asked to present her final statement in court.

The presiding judge, Zeng Hanzhou, sternly warned Jiang Qing that she was committing a new offence in slandering and vilifying Party and state leaders. He said that the court had held six sessions to investigate prosecution's charges against Jiang Qing, and carefully examined all documentary and parol evidence relevant to the case. The presiding judge pointed out, "the tribunal gave Jiang Qing enough time to defend herself. However, she chose to evade the issue and present arguments irrelevant to and out of the scope of the charges in the indictment; besides she made use of the debate to make new counter-revolutionary remarks.

"While presenting her final statement, Jiang Qing continued to vilify Party and state leaders, smear the bench, and slander the prosecutors. The Special Court, in line with its duty and in accordance with the law, will not let go her criminal liability," the presiding judge concluded.

ZHANG CHUNQIAO: SILENT THROUGHOUT

The prosecutor declared during the court debate on December 20 that Zhang Chunqiao had kept silent and shown a "defiant attitude" throughout the trial and refused to acknowledge his crimes in the face of overwhelming evidence.

The prosecutor, Ma Chunyi, said in his statement that Zhang Chunqiao had said in Shanghai early in 1967 that "our aim in the great proletarian cultural revolution has always been to seize power, from the grass roots to the central organizations, including powers of the Party, the government, as well as in the financial, cultural and other fields."

"Change of Dynasty" — The Gang's Programme

Ma Chunyi also quoted Zhang as saying "we must seize power everywhere" and added that on a number of other occasions Zhang had said the cultural revolution meant "a change of dynasty."

Zhang regarded veteran cadres as serious obstacles to their usurpation of Party and state power. Zhang had said: "All of them are bad" and "none shall be spared."

The prosecutor said that Zhang's words had become the programme of action for the Gang of Four. During the "cultural revolution" they had falsely accused and persecuted Party and state leaders and suppressed the cadres.

Ma Chunyi said that those framed and persecuted included Liu Shaoqi (late State Chairman), Zhu De (late Chairman of the Standing Committee of the National People's Congress), Chen Yi (late Vice-Premier), Ye Jianying (now Chairman of the N.P.C. Standing Committee), and also Vice-Premiers Li Xiannian, Chen Yun, Nie Rongzhen, Li Fuchun and Tan Zhenlin.

The prosecutor told the court that in October 1974 Chang Chunqiao, together with the other members of the Gang of Four, made false charges against Deng Xiaoping, now Vice-Chairman of the Party Central Committee.

On April 5, 1976, the prosecutor said, Zhang false-
ly accused Deng of being China's "Nagy," using the April
protest demonstrations against the Gang of Four in Tian
An Men Square as the basis of the accusation. Prosecutor
Ma said this accusation was the signal for overthrowing
Deng Xiaoping a second time.

Ma Chunyi said that at the instigation of Zhang Chunqiao and other members of the Gang of Four, the Mayor
and Vice-Mayor of Shanghai, Cao Diqiu and Jin Zhonghua, were persecuted to death.

During the period 1967-68, Zhang Chunqiao organized
and personally controlled a special espionage group (code-
named 244), the prosecutor said. The group undertook
taking people into custody and secretly interrogating and
torturing them to extort confession.

The prosecutor said that on December 28, 1966 Zhang
Chunqiao instructed Wang Hongwen and others to create
an armed clash in Shanghai, causing 91 casualties. Zhang
and Yao Wenyuan on May 7, 1967 instigated another armed clash in Ji'nan, the provincial capital of Shandong.
In this incident, 388 people were unlawfully arrested.

Ma Chunyi said: "Defendant Zhang Chunqiao fully
understood the importance of the gun-barrel in realizing
his ambition to usurp Party and state power. He collaborated with Wang Hongwen to establish an armed force
under their control in the early part of the 'cultural revolution.' He was the principal instigator of the Shanghai
armed rebellion in October 1976."

Twice Asked to Make a Final Statement

After Ma Chunyi's statement, Judge Zeng Hanzhou
twice asked Zhang Chunqiao: "Have you anything to say
in your defence?" Zhang did not answer. After waiting
for two minutes, the judge said: "The defendant did not

110

make any statement; his reticence will be entered in the court record."

Judge Zeng, in closing the debate, again told Zhang that he had the right to make a final statement. When Zhang again refused to answer, the judge told him to await the verdict of the court.

YAO WENYUAN: ADMITTING "MISTAKES"

During the court debate on December 19, Yao Wenyuan declared that he would not argue facts he had already acknowledged. However, he denied a number of charges, among them incitement through the mass media to frame Party and state leaders and to overthrow the proletarian dictatorship.

Prosecutor Zhong Shuqin told the court that during the "cultural revolution," Yao Wenyuan, who controlled the mass media, took an active part in the plot of the Lin Biao and Jiang Qing cliques to overthrow the proletarian dictatorship and socialist system. He said Yao was a principal conspirator and the clique's mouthpiece.

Crimes, Not Mistakes

Yao Wenyuan, reading a statement on his own behalf, told the court: "I still hold to my words on the facts I have already acknowledged, and I am not going to argue further on these facts." He denied that it was through him that the Lin Biao and Jiang Qing cliques used the mass media for incitement to overthrow the proletarian dictatorship. He said that in the press articles he handled

111

"not all the veteran cadres at all levels in the Party and government" were attacked. The articles attacked "only some of them."

He also said that when he branded mourners at Tian An Men Square in April 1976 as "counter-revolutionaries" and "bad elements" he was merely committing a mistake.

Prosecutor Wang Wenlin said Yao Wenyuan's defence was "entirely unacceptable." He added: "It is in short an admission of making mistakes and a denial of criminal offence."

The prosecutor said that in previous court investigations Yao Wenyuan tried to present so-called "historical conditions" as a basis for his defence.

He said: "We must refute Yao Wenyuan's argument that all his deeds in the ten years of the 'cultural revolution' were legal." It was in those ten years of chaos that Yao Wenyuan climbed from membership of the *Liberation Daily* editorial board in Shanghai to membership of the Party Central Committee and its Political Bureau. Yao Wenyuan used his ill-gotten status and power to control the mass media and made counter-revolutionary propaganda to pave the way for the Gang of Four to usurp Party and state power and overthrow the political power of the proletarian dictatorship. "These are the actual 'historical conditions.'"

Prosecutor Wang said it was in these actual historical conditions that Yao Wenyuan accused through the mass media veteran revolutionaries of being "bourgeois democrats," "capitalist roaders who are still on the road," "restorationist maniacs," "restorationist legions," "imperialist flunkeys," and "traitors." "What is this, if not an attempt to overthrow the proletarian dictatorship and socialist system?"

He said: "Yao Wenyuan accused intellectuals and others of being bad elements, gangsters, counter-revolutionaries, a social foundation for counter-revolution and reactionary academic authorities; he further urged brutal suppression and executions. What are these, if not moves to harm the People's Republic of China?"

Lawyers' Defence

Defence lawyers Han Xuezhang and Zhang Zhong told the court that it could not be established that Yao Wenyuan was involved in a plot by two other members of the Gang of Four, Zhang Chunqiao and Wang Hongwen, to stage an armed rebellion in Shanghai in October 1976 as charged.

The lawyers recalled Yao Wenyuan's discussions with one of the followers of the Gang of Four who had come to the capital from Shanghai in May 1976, in which Yao said that the "cultural revolution" was a form of violence and that in the future things would still be settled by violence.

They said these remarks could not be counted as "preparing public opinion for the armed rebellion in Shanghai." Yao Wenyuan was speaking at a time when the Beijing Tian An Men demonstration against the Gang of Four had already been crushed by the Gang who were then "dizzy with success." The defence lawyers said Yao at that time could not have known that the Gang would fall in October 1976 and he would have had no reason to plot an armed rebellion in Shanghai. They said that there was no link between Yao's statements and the rebellion and that "Yao Wenyuan should not bear criminal liability for it."

The defence lawyers also noted that some of Yao Wenyuan's offences were committed under the instructions of Jiang Qing, who headed the Gang of Four. In the instance of plotting to frame the late Premier Zhou Enlai and Vice-Premier Deng Xiaoping, Yao Wenyuan was one of the participants in the plot and "should, of course, bear a certain degree of responsibility." However, there were important differences between Yao's responsibility and that of the principal instigator, Jiang Qing, the lawyers argued.

Yao should also bear partial responsibility for framing the Shanghai municipal Party committee which led to the deaths of Cao Diqiu and Jin Zhonghua, then Mayor and Vice-Mayor, the lawyers said. However, they added, it was Zhang Chunqiao who played the main and decisive role in this.

As for responsibility for the violence in Ji'nan on May 7, 1967, the lawyers said, the evidence already produced before the court showed that Zhang Chunqiao should be the one to bear the chief responsibility.

WANG HONGWEN: PLEADING GUILTY

Wang Hongwen declared during the court debate on December 20 that he was guilty of all charges against him, and he requested a chance to reform.

"The abundant evidence has shown that the crimes committed by the Lin Biao and Jiang Qing counter-revolutionary cliques are exceptionally grave," said Wang Hongwen in his final statement. "As one of the principal defendants, I admit I have also committed a number of serious crimes. I should admit this honestly before the people of the whole country. I hope the court will give me a chance to repent and reform myself."

At the same December 20 session, the prosecution told the court that the state had produced ample evidence to show that Wang Hongwen and the other members of the Gang of Four framed and persecuted Party and state leaders Zhou Enlai (the late Premier), Deng Xiaoping (now Vice-Chairman of the Central Committee of the Chinese Communist Party), and Chen Yi (the late Vice-Premier).

The prosecution said Wang Hongwen built up an armed force in Shanghai and, on the eve of the downfall of the Gang of Four in 1976, plotted an armed rebellion there. Wang also engineered and directed an armed attack on the mass organization of the Shanghai Diesel Engine Plant and another armed clash known as the Kangping Road Incident.

After listing Wang's other crimes, the prosecution called the court's attention to the fact that he had pleaded guilty and to some degree had repented and showed willingness to submit to the law.

CHEN BODA: REQUESTING LENIENCY

Chen Boda admitted during the court debate on December 18 that he was guilty of framing and persecuting former State Chairman Liu Shaoqi and former Central Committee Political Bureau Alternate Member Lu Dingyi.

Making his final statement before the First Tribunal, Chen Boda also admitted full responsibility for fabricating a case against the Party organization of eastern Hebei Province which affected tens of thousands of people and resulted in 2,955 deaths.

"I plead guilty," Chen Boda said. "I have nothing to say to defend myself." Chen then requested leniency from the court.

Chen Boda also revealed that Jiang Qing had asked him to recommend her as an advisor to the "cultural revolution group" of the Military Commission of the Party Central

Committee. Chen Boda then made the suggestion to Ye Qun, wife of Lin Biao, and Lin Biao promptly appointed Jiang Qing to the post. Chen Boda said Ye Qun had told him that Jiang Qing was very ambitious and that her aim was not simply to be an advisor but to acquire leadership of the whole army.

Chen Boda said that after he learned of the power struggle between Lin Biao and Jiang Qing, he sympathized with Lin Biao. But he said he saw through Jiang Qing's ambitious nature only gradually.

Prosecutor Qu Wenda said that the evidence against Chen Boda was conclusive: Chen Boda actively participated in the Lin Biao and Jiang Qing counter-revolutionary cliques in scheming to usurp Party and state power and to overthrow the People's Republic and the socialist system. As a chief culprit of the Lin Biao and Jiang Qing groups, Chen Boda caused grievous harm to the Party, state and people and violated several articles of the Criminal Law, Qu Wenda said.

"His crime is grave," said the prosecutor. "I suggest the Special Court mete out due punishment to him appropriate to his crime."

Lawyers' View

Defence lawyers Gan Yupei and Fu Zhiren, speaking on Chen Boda's behalf, also found the evidence conclusive. Speaking for both, Gan Yupei said, "It is our view that Chen Boda did play a prime role in taking the decision to castigate and persecute Liu Shaoqi."

The lawyer continued, however, that Chen Boda was only one of several major figures involved in attacking Liu Shaoqi, and "his position and role were different from those of Lin Biao, Jiang Qing, Kang Sheng and Zhang Chunqiao."

116

The lawyer also said that Chen Boda should "bear an unshirkable responsibility" for fabricating the eastern Hebei Province case. "However," he went on, "the consequence that tens of thousands of people were framed and persecuted and thousands were killed or injured was not due to his words alone. In fact, there were other factors which cannot be overlooked. Chen Boda should therefore bear a certain amount of responsibility but not the entire onus for the serious consequences."

On the question of the defendant's attitude, Gan Yupei noted that Chen Boda had pleaded guilty, admitted repeatedly in court that his crimes were "grave," assumed responsibility for his crimes and said he would accept due punishment. Chen Boda's attitude, said the lawyer, should be a factor for leniency.

HUANG YONGSHENG: DENYING ROLE
AS CHIEF CULPRIT

The court debate on the charges against Huang Yongsheng occupied three sessions from December 18 to December 20. The debate centred around the question whether the accused was a "principal culprit" or "an ordinary member" of the Lin Biao clique. Huang Yongsheng spoke for some three hours in his own defence. His arguments were refuted by prosecutors Zhang Zhongru and Zhu Zongzheng.

Enumerating facts to show Huang Yongsheng's important position in the Lin Biao clique, prosecutor Zhang said that the defendant had played a major role in framing and persecuting Party and state leaders, engineering the overthrow of the dictatorship of the proletariat and hastening Lin Biao's decision to stage an armed coup and assassinate Chairman Mao Zedong.

Zhang Zhongru said that Huang Yongsheng was guilty of plotting to subvert the government and split the country and of organizing and directing a counter-revolutionary clique.

Defending himself, Huang Yongsheng denied having anything to do with Lin Biao's plot to assassinate Chairman Mao in September 1971. He said he had never been aware of it, still less participated in plotting or carrying out the project. So, he said, he was only an ordinary member of Lin Biao's counter-revolutionary clique and not a principal culprit.

Prosecution Refutes Huang

Refuting Huang Yongsheng's arguments, prosecutor Zhu Zongzheng said that in September 1970, when the Lin Biao counter-revolutionary clique had failed in its plot to usurp Party and state power through a "peaceful transition" in Lushan, Huang Yongsheng did everything in his power to cover up Lin Biao's crimes.

The prosecutor said that several days before Lin Biao defected on September 13, 1971, he wrote a confidential letter to Huang Yongsheng, telling Huang: "If you have any problems, consult Comrade Wang Fei directly." Wang Fei was responsible for operations in Beijing in the projected coup d'etat.

On September 6, 1971, Huang Yongsheng secretly reported to Lin Biao and Ye Qun about Chairman Mao Zedong's talks directed against them during his inspection tour of southern China, thus prompting Lin Biao to decide to assassinate Chairman Mao.

Zhu Zongzheng further pointed out that Huang Yongsheng framed and persecuted Party and state leaders including Ye Jianying, Nie Rongzhen, Peng Dehuai and Luo Ruiqing, senior military officers, and Party and government leaders in Guangdong Province. All these acts were deliberate counter-revolutionary offences.

The prosecutor said that in the offences jointly committed by members of the Lin Biao clique, Huang Yongsheng played a major role as an organizer and leader and therefore was a principal culprit in the clique.

Pinpointing Huang Yongsheng's denial of facts and his refusal to admit his guilt in spite of conclusive evidence, the prosecutor Zhang Zhongru asked the court to take this into consideration in meting out punishment.

WU FAXIAN: "I HATE MYSELF"

"I hate myself, I hate the traitor and renegade Lin Biao. . . . I brought calamity and caused losses to the Party, the state, the people and the army. I take responsibility for the serious crimes I committed," said Wu Faxian on December 18 in a debate on the charges brought against him in the indictment.

"I plead guilty without reserve, submit myself to the law completely, and subject myself to the judgement handed down by the court," he also said.

Wu Faxian admitted that the basic reason for his crimes was that he "harboured counter-revolutionary ambitions." "I wanted to climb to the top by following in the footsteps of Lin Biao," he added. "As a result, I got more and more deeply involved to the point of committing serious crimes."

After enumerating Wu Faxian's offences, prosecutor Sun Shufeng said: "The defendant Wu Faxian, followed Lin Biao zealously and pursued over a long period counter-revolutionary criminal activities. . . . He acted as an organizer and leader in the Lin Biao counter-revolutionary clique."

Wu Faxian said that he had nothing to argue with the prosecutor. He said that the prosecutor's statement was "factual and realistic, supported by witnesses' testimony and documentary evidence."

Advocates Ask for Leniency

Ma Kechang and Zhou Hengyuan, the advocates for Wu Faxian, made a joint statement in his defence, which said: "The case of the Lin Biao and Jiang Qing counter-revolutionary cliques is an offence jointly committed by a group of persons. The principal members of these cliques should bear criminal liability for the offences they plotted or committed, but not for those they did not plan or commit."

As charged in the indictment, the statement said, Wu Faxian should be held responsible for illicitly placing the command of the Air Force in the hands of Lin Biao's son, Lin Liguo, enabling the young Lin to carry out counter-revolutionary activities. But, at that time, Wu Faxian was not aware of the offences committed by Lin Liguo in preparing for an armed coup d'etat and therefore cannot bear direct responsibility for these offences. (Wu said earlier in court that he should bear direct responsibility).

As regards the offence specified in the indictment that Lin Biao and Ye Qun planned to "flee south to Guangzhou," taking along Wu Faxian and others, and "to set up a separate party central committee there to split the nation," Wu Faxian was not aware of it either.

The statement said: "We appeal to the Special Court to give full consideration to the above facts in determining Wu Faxian's criminal liability.

"Wu Faxian is one of the principal defendants in this case and we have no objection to this. But he is not the chief criminal among the principal offenders.

"It is true that Wu Faxian committed serious crimes in framing and persecuting proletarian revolutionaries of the older generation and that he should bear criminal liability for this. However, many of his offences in this regard were committed under the instructions of Lin Biao and Ye Qun. We ask the court to give appropriate consideration to this circumstance in determining Wu Faxian's criminal liability."

The defence lawyers also mentioned in their statement that Wu Faxian had time and again pleaded guilty, shown readiness to submit to the law, expressed his wish to turn over a new leaf and atone for his crimes.

The statement noted that Wu Faxian provided materials exposing Lin Biao, Jiang Qing, Ye Qun, Huang Yongsheng, Li Zuopeng and Qiu Huizuo. Court investigation and examination showed that his disclosures proved to be generally accurate.

"Wu Faxian's attitude is relatively good in pleading guilty and showing repentance. We hereby ask the Special Court to take into consideration his fairly good behaviour in meting out punishment.

"We hope that, in line with the policy of combining punishment with leniency as described in Article 1 of the Criminal Law, the Special Court will take into consideration the above-mentioned mitigating circumstances in accordance with the law, and lighten the penalty when passing judgement on the defendant Wu Faxian," the lawyers' statement concluded.

LI ZUOPENG: "BASICALLY" ACCEPTING INDICTMENT

A debate on the charges against Li Zuopeng was held on December 22. Prosecutor Zhang Zhaoqi pointed out that Li Zuopeng had actively participated in the counter-revolutionary activities of the Lin Biao counter-revolutionary clique aimed at overthrowing the dictatorship of the proletariat and the socialist system and usurping supreme Party leadership and state power. Li Zuopeng's crimes were serious.

Zhang Zhaoqi focused particularly on the counter-revolutionary nature of Li Zuopeng's collusion with Lin Biao, "who invariably used Li as a shock force at crucial moments." Li Zuopeng served Lin Biao by hurling groundless charges at Party and state leaders for the purpose of overthrowing them. Li Zuopeng personally framed more than 120 cadres in the Navy, three of whom were subsequently persecuted to death.

Li Zuopeng admitted in the court debate that he had committed crimes in framing veteran revolutionaries He Long, Ye Jianying and Luo Ruiqing, and that he was responsible for framing and persecuting a large number of cadres and others in the Navy during the "cultural revolution."

As for tampering with Premier Zhou Enlai's instructions on September 13, 1971, that Lin Biao's special plane must not be allowed to take off without an order given jointly by four leading officials, an act which enabled Lin Biao to flee the country, Li Zuopeng said that he had formerly admitted only to having committed a mistake, not an offence. "Now I not only admit this as a mistake but also as a crime," Li Zuopeng said.

As regards the framing and persecution of Navy cadres, Li Zuopeng said: "This was a very complicated matter and . . . I request the court to consider carefully if I should be held directly responsible for them." He then contradicted himself about tampering with Premier Zhou Enlai's instructions concerning the take-off of Lin Biao's special plane, saying: "I admit the offence conditionally."

Advocates' Statement

In their joint statement in defence of Li Zuopeng, the advocates Zhang Sizhi and Su Huiyu raised no objection to the charge that he was "one of the principal culprits of the Lin Biao counter-revolutionary clique."

Li Zuopeng bore definite responsibility for the joint offence of the clique. However, the lawyers noted, he did not participate in drawing up the *Outline of "Project 571,"* the programme for the armed coup, as shown in the court investigations. Nor was there any evidence to show that the defendant participated in planning to flee south to Guangzhou and set up a separate party central committee there as charged in the indictment, the statement said.

The advocates held that some of the offences Li Zuopeng was charged with, including the framing of Luo Ruiqing, the former Chief of General Staff of the People's Liberation Army, and the persecution of a large number of Navy officers, were committed on Lin Biao's instructions or advice.

The advocates appealed to the court to take into consideration the differences involved in the above circumstances in pursuing criminal liability against Li Zuopeng. They also mentioned the initiative taken by Li Zuopeng in revealing his own offences.

Making his final plea at the conclusion of the debate, Li Zuopeng again tried to defend himself on the points he had raised during the debate. But he admitted he had committed serious offences in framing Ye Jianying, He Long and Luo Ruiqing. "The charges listed in the indictment against me are basically true, but not entirely true. Therefore, I accept them basically," Li Zuopeng said.

QIU HUIZUO: "ALWAYS CONSIDER MYSELF GUILTY"

On December 20, 1980 a debate was held on the charges against Qiu Huizuo.

Prosecutor Wang Pusheng said in a statement in court that Qiu Huizuo actively followed Lin Biao in framing and persecuting state leaders and leading members of the General Political Department of the People's Liberation Army. Qiu set up illegal prisons in the General Logistics Department to extort confessions through torture. He personally framed 462 people, of whom eight were persecuted to death.

Prosecutor Wang Pusheng said: "We suggest that, in accordance with the provisions of Article 1 of the Criminal Law on combining punishment and leniency, the court take into consideration, while meting out punishment, the fairly good attitude of the defendant Qiu Huizuo, in admitting his guilt."

In closing his final remarks, Qiu Huizuo pleaded guilty in the form of a written statement read out in court. In it he said: "The court investigation of my offences was realistic and fair. I came to see my crimes more clearly during the course of the investigation. I committed crimes and should be subjected to trial and legal sanctions. The trial I have been submitted to is a correct measure to enforce law and discipline and uphold justice.

"I unreservedly plead guilty and will always consider myself guilty.

"I will submit completely to the judgement to be handed down by the Special Court. I will try my best to see my crimes and accept the judgement consciously, and will never break the law again. My crimes are historical facts which are unalterable but, as a man, I can turn over a new leaf. I am determined to continue reforming myself."

———◆———

JIANG TENGJIAO: READY TO ATONE FOR CRIMES

A court debate on the charges against Jiang Tengjiao was conducted on December 1, 1980.

Prosecutor Tu Men pointed out that Jiang Tengjiao played a main role and was an organizer and leader in the Lin Biao counter-revolutionary clique's plot to assassinate Chairman Mao, stage an armed counter-revolutionary coup and split the state.

Defence Pleas

Wang Shunhua and Zhou Kuizheng, defence counsels for Jiang Tengjiao, then presented their arguments.

Wang Shunhua said: "We hold that the offence committed by Jiang Tengjiao in taking an active part in the conspiracy to assassinate Chairman Mao Zedong and engineer the flight south to Guangzhou as charged in the indictment is explicit and has been proved by conclusive evidence. We have no objection to it."

However, on the basis of study of the prosecution's evidence relevant to the case, the two advocates made the following pleas:

First. In the case of the Lin Biao and Jiang Qing counter-revolutionary cliques, Lin Biao and Jiang Qing were the chief culprits and should bear the main responsibility for the crimes committed by the cliques. It was at Lin Biao's personal instigation and Lin Liguo's personal command that the accused Jiang Tengjiao committed the serious crimes mentioned above. There was some difference between Jiang Tengjiao and the chief criminal, Lin Biao, and the principal culprit, Lin Liguo, in respect of their criminal liability.

Second. Regarding the charge that the defendant had searched the homes of Shanghai film and opera artists and then sent the materials so obtained to Beijing, this crime was plotted jointly by Jiang Qing and Ye Qun.

Third. Jiang Tengjiao confessed his offences fairly promptly. Lin Biao and company defected on September 13, 1971. When the authorities talked with Jiang Tengjiao the following day, he was still unaware that Lin Biao had died in Mongolia, but he voluntarily confessed quite a number of his offences. He also wrote "details on the event of plotting to assassinate Chairman Mao," and exposed of his own accord the offences committed by Lin Biao, Ye Qun, Lin Liguo and others. This helped uncover the facts in the case. Shortly afterwards, the defendant made another confession about the secret meeting called by Lin Liguo in Shanghai on March 31, 1971. In general, Jiang Tengjiao's confessions tallied with the facts.

Showing Repentance

Moreover, the counsel Wang Shunhua said, Jiang Tengjiao showed repentance during the court hearings. In recent talks with his lawyers, Jiang Tengjiao had again stated that "first, I should be tried and punished by the people; second, the indictment is factual and realistic." Jiang also said: "I plead guilty and submit to the law."

Wang Shunhua further said that Jiang Tengjiao had expressed the hope that he would be given a chance to atone for his crime. "As his advocates, we have the responsibility to present his request to the court for consideration." "We have put forward the above opinions in his defence, and we hope the court will give a lighter sentence in view of the mitigating circumstances."

In presenting his final statement Jiang Tengjiao said: "I am weighed down with serious crimes and the evidence is irrefutable. I bow my head in confession of my crimes and submission to the law. I am ready to accept whatever punishment is due me."

COURT JUDGEMENT

THE TRIAL CONCLUDES

After lasting a total of 67 days, the trial of the Lin Biao and Jiang Qing counter-revolutionary cliques concluded on January 25, 1981. The judgement on Jiang Qing and nine other defendants was announced at the Special Court.

Jiang Qing was sentenced to death with a two-year reprieve and permanent deprivation of political rights;

Zhang Chunqiao was sentenced to death with a two-year reprieve and permanent deprivation of political rights;

Yao Wenyuan: 20 years' imprisonment and deprivation of political rights for five years;

Wang Hongwen: life imprisonment and permanent deprivation of political rights;

Chen Boda: 18 years' imprisonment and deprivation of political rights for five years;

Huang Yongsheng: 18 years' imprisonment and deprivation of political rights for five years;

Wu Faxian: 17 years' imprisonment and deprivation of political rights for five years;

Li Zuopeng: 17 years' imprisonment and deprivation of political rights for five years;

Qiu Huizuo: 16 years' imprisonment and deprivation of political rights for five years;

Jiang Tengjiao: 18 years' imprisonment and deprivation of political rights for five years.

At nine o'clock in the morning of January 25 after Jiang Hua, President of the Special Court, declared the session open, the ten defendants were led to the dock. The reading of the judgement* ended at 10:45. Jiang Qing and Zhang Chunqiao were handcuffed by court police immediately after their sentences were announced. Towards the end of the session, Jiang Qing repeatedly called out and disrupted the order of the court. Wu Xiuquan who presided over the session, ordered that she be taken away from the courtroom.

The court judgement read out by Jiang Hua stressed that the criminal activities of the two cliques lasted for a whole decade, bringing calamities to all fields of work and all parts of the country, seriously jeopardizing the people's democratic dictatorship and socialist public order, inflicting very great damage upon the national economy and all other undertakings, and causing enormous disasters for the people of all the nationalities in the country.

The judgement declared: "This court has held a total of 42 sessions for investigation and debate, during which 49 witnesses and victims appeared in court to testify, and 873 pieces of evidence were examined." The offences committed by the two cliques "have been verified by great amounts of material and documentary evidence, conclusions of expert corroboration, testimonies of witnesses and statements of victims. The facts are clear and the evidence conclusive."

After listing in details the specific criminal liability of each defendant, the judgement pointed out that Jiang Qing had acted as a ringleader. She bore direct or indirect responsibilities for all the offences by the counter-revolutionary clique she organized and led. In view of the seriousness of the damage she had caused the country and the people, her case was particularly odious.

---

* See page 199 for full text of the judgement.

Zhang Chunqiao, the judgement continued, collaborated with Jiang Qing in organizing and leading a counter-revolutionary clique. During the decade of turmoil, he continuously initiated and instigated plots to usurp the people's democratic power. He therefore caused extremely grave harm to the state and people.

The judgement stated that the sentences were final and that "the fixed term of imprisonment for those who are sentenced to such a penalty shall run from the first day of enforcement of the sentence. Where an offender has been held in prior custody, the duration of such custody shall be deducted from the term of imprisonment at the rate of one day for each day spent in prior custody."

After reading out the judgement Jiang Hua ordered that the convicts be led out for the enforcement of the sentences. Then at 10:50 a.m. he announced the conclusion of the court, drawing thunderous applause from the 1,200 representatives in the gallery.

The court sessions were attended by a total of more than 60,000 people from all parts of the country.

ARTICLES OF CHINA'S CRIMINAL LAW RELEVANT TO THE JUDGEMENT OF THE LIN-JIANG CASE

Article 90 Any act which jeopardizes the People's Republic of China for the purpose of overthrowing the political power of the dictatorship of the proletariat and overthrowing the socialist system is a counter-revolutionary offence.

Article 92 Whoever conspires to overthrow the government or split the state shall be sentenced to life imprisonment or to imprisonment for not less than ten years.

Article 93 Whoever instigates, seduces or buys over any state functionary or any member of the armed forces, the people's police or the militia to go over to the enemy and turn traitor, or to rebel treacherously, shall be sentenced to life imprisonment or to imprisonment for not less than ten years.

Article 98 Whoever organizes or leads a counter-revolutionary group shall be sentenced to imprisonment for not less than five years; other active participants in such a group shall be sentenced to imprisonment for not more than five years, or to detention, or to public surveillance, or to deprivation of political rights.

Article 101 Whoever kills or injures a person by poisoning, spreading disease germs or by other means for the purpose of counter-revolution shall be sentenced to life imprisonment or to imprisonment for not less than ten years or, in less serious cases, to imprisonment for from three to ten years.

Article 102 Whoever commits any of the following acts for the purpose of counter-revolution shall be sentenced to imprisonment for not more than five years, or to detention, or to public surveillance, or to deprivation of political rights; chief offenders, or any others who commit any such offences in serious degree, shall be sentenced to imprisonment for not less than five years:

(1) Inciting the masses to resist or sabotage the implementation of any law or decree; and

(2) Inciting others to overthrow the state power of the dictatorship of the proletariat and the socialist system through counter-revolutionary posters or leaflets or by other means.

Article 103 Whoever commits any of the counter-revolutionary offences specified in this chapter, with the exception of Articles 98, 99 and 102, and causes particularly grave harm to the state and the people in a particularly flagrant case may be sentenced to death.

Article 138 Persecution of a cadre or any common citizen on a false charge by any means whatsoever shall be strictly prohibited. Whoever fabricates facts to bring a false charge against another person (including a convict in prison), shall be subject to criminal sanction in the light of the nature, seriousness and consequences of the offence of fabricated charge and in accordance with the prescribed penalty for such an offence. A state functionary found guilty of bringing a false charge against another person shall be punished more heavily.

The provisions of the preceding paragraph do not apply to a person who institutes charges against another person mistakenly rather than makes a deliberate frame-up or provides misinformation against him.

Article 20 An attempt is where the commission of an offence is begun but not consummated for reasons beyond the offender's control.

The penalty for an attempt may be lighter or be mitigated in comparison with that for a consummated offence.

Article 43 The death penalty shall be imposed only on offenders who have committed the most heinous crimes. Where immediate execution is not deemed necessary, an offender whose offence warrants a death sentence, may be sentenced to death with a two-year reprieve to be announced at the same time so as to reform him through labour and see how he will behave.

With the exception of those handed down by the Supreme People's Court pursuant to law, all death sentences shall be submitted to the Supreme People's Court for examination and approval. A death sentence with reprieve may be handed down by a higher people's court or may become final after its examination and approval.

Article 52 Counter-revolutionaries shall be deprived of political rights; where necessary, offenders guilty of seriously disrupting public order may also be deprived of such rights.

Article 53 An offender sentenced to death or life imprisonment shall be permanently deprived of political rights.

Where a death sentence with reprieve, or a sentence of life imprisonment, is reduced to fixed-term imprisonment, the period of deprivation of political rights shall be converted to a term from three years to ten years.

Article 64 With the exception of those sentenced to death or to life imprisonment, offenders who have committed several offences prior to judgement are liable to a compound penalty, the period of which shall be no longer than the sum of the periods of the individual penalties nor shorter than the longest among them, to be decided at the discretion of the court. However, the period of the compound penalty shall not exceed three years if the penalty is public surveillance, nor exceed one year if the penalty is detention, nor exceed 20 years if the penalty is fixed-term imprisonment.

The supplementary penalty imposed for any of the several offences shall still be enforced.

Article 76 No prosecution shall be instituted after the following periods have elapsed subsequent to the commission of an offence:

(1) Five years for offences for which the maximum prescribed penalty is imprisonment for below five years;

(2) Ten years for offences for which the maximum prescribed penalty is imprisonment for not less than five years but below ten years;

(3) Fifteen years for offences for which the maximum prescribed penalty is imprisonment for not less than ten years; and

(4) Twenty years for offences for which the maximum prescribed penalty is life imprisonment or death; where,

after the elapse of twenty years, it is still deemed necessary to prosecute, the matter shall first be submitted to the supreme people's procuratorate for examination and approval.

The Criminal Law came into force on January 1, 1980. Article 9 of this law stipulates: "If an act performed after the founding of the People's Republic of China and prior to the enforcement of the present law was not deemed an offence under the laws, decrees and policies then in force, these laws, decrees and policies shall be the standard. If the act was deemed an offence under the said laws, decrees and policies and is also subject to prosecution under Section VIII, Chapter Four, of the General Provisions of the present law, the standard of criminal liability shall also be the said laws, decrees and policies. But if the act is not deemed an offence or the penalty for the offence is lighter under the present law, the present law shall apply."

———————◆———————

COMMENTS

MILESTONE IN SOCIALIST DEMOCRACY AND SOCIALIST LEGALITY

— **Main Points of an Article by** *People's Daily*
Special Commentator Published on
December 22, 1980

Some people may ask why wait more than four years after the fall of the Gang of Four before bringing the Lin Biao and Jiang Qing cliques to trial. The answer is that time was needed to unravel the skeins of a very complicated situation lasting ten chaotic years.

The two cliques were counter-revolutionary cliques and they had emerged during the "cultural revolution," and the chief figures, using double-dealing tactics, acted in the name of the Party and government leaders. The "cultural revolution" itself was complicated and this complicated matters more. Time and effort were needed to do the enormous amount of work of investigation, analyzing carefully and weighing up facts. Even for the principal figures of the two cliques, their offences had to be clearly and factually established to determine whether they had broken the law or had violated Party discipline, before they could be punished.

The public trial was to establish their criminal liability, not to bring in any errors in work, including errors of political line.

Distinguishing Crimes from Mistakes

Generally speaking it is difficult not to commit errors in work or even go wrong in political line, and that includes all revolutionary parties and leading personnel as well. Time and again in the history of our Party there have been errors in political line. Those were mistakes made along the difficult and protracted road of struggle in the revolutionary interests of the nation and the Party, mistakes resulting from a departure from objective reality and from the fundamental principles of Marxism.

A clear demarcation line must be drawn between errors of this kind and crimes of a counter-revolutionary nature. This is a long-standing policy of our Party, tested and proved in practice to be correct.

Comrade Mao Zedong in his later years made mistakes, especially in the years of the "cultural revolution," which he started and led. These mistakes brought grave misfortune to the Party and the people. Of course he was not the only one in the Party to make mistakes; other comrades also made mistakes. However, the nature of these mistakes is entirely different from the underhanded activities of the Lin Biao and Jiang Qing counter-revolutionary cliques.

What are the fundamental differences between the crimes committed by the members of the Lin-Jiang cliques and the mistakes made by others? We can look at the question from three aspects:

First, they are different in nature. An error stems from misinterpreting the objective world and from an action that does not conform to objective reality. A crime is another matter. It is an action punishable by law. According to the Criminal Law of China, activities directed at subverting the government, dividing the country, instigating rebellions, killing and inflicting bodily harm to people for counter-revolutionary purposes, etc., are counter-revolutionary crimes.

Second, the means employed are different. Lin Biao, Jiang Qing and their close collaborators resorted to every conceivable means, fair or foul, to achieve their aim of usurping Party and state leadership. Apart from plotting political murder, coup d'etat and rebellion, they also used every means to frame Party and state leaders and to suppress cadres and the masses. They concocted evidence, extorted confessions by torture, organized spies and agents, and they seized and incarcerated innocent people, beat them up, looted and ransacked houses and stirred up armed strife among the people. These are all criminal acts prohibited by China's Criminal Law. Obviously, there is a marked difference between such actions and mistakes, including mistakes of political line, committed by people acting through normal organizational channels, work procedures and methods.

Thirdly, committing errors in work and committing counter-revolutionary crimes differ from each other as regards their objectives. The former, generally speaking, arises out of good intentions to serve the revolution, while the latter is carried out for definite counter-revolutionary objectives.

Facts as Basis and Law the Sole Criterion

That the people detest and hate the two cliques is natural, considering the enormity of their crimes, the great number of people victimized and the damage they did to the nation. Seldom in China and anywhere else in the world have such destructiveness and suffering been imposed on so many. But the trial was conducted strictly according to the principles of socialist democracy,

137

the judicial system and procedures. It will withstand the test of time and review by future generations.

The principle of independence of judicial work was implemented throughout the trial. Though many of the complicated details had been investigated by the Party earlier, they were re-investigated and re-examined by the governmental public security organizations. The case was referred to the people's procuratorate for prosecution and then submitted to the people's court. The Special Court consisted of 35 judges, most of them experienced, professional judges, plus a small number of non-professionals, who also acted as a jury to present the views of ordinary people.

The principle of democracy was implemented throughout. In accordance with the Law of Criminal Procedure, an open trial was conducted. Representatives from all walks of life attended the court hearings. But as the trial involved state secrets, foreign observers could not attend. The defendants had full right to defend themselves; they could plead their own case or have defence lawyers to act in their behalf.

The whole court procedure was carried out by taking facts as the basis and the law as the sole criterion. According to China's Law of Criminal Procedure, "No accused shall be adjudged guilty and sentenced without evidence other than his confession; he shall be convicted and punished if there is sufficient evidence against him even without his confession."

Furthermore, the principle of revolutionary humanitarianism was applied. The trial of Lin-Jiang cliques was held according to the new Criminal Law instead of the Regulations Governing the Punishment of Counter-Revolutionaries promulgated in 1951 which would have meted out harsher sentences.

The trial also fully accorded with the principle that "everyone is equal before the law." Although all ten defendants had been "big shots," they could not escape the law. In socialist China, no one shall be a privileged citizen standing above the law.

The trial of the two counter-revolutionary cliques and the principles followed in the trial proclaimed that the Chinese people are clearing away the dregs of history and forging ahead along the road of democracy and rule by law.

INTERVIEWS WITH NOTED JURISTS

Answers by Zhang Youyu

Jurist Zhang Youyu, 82, Vice-President of the Chinese Academy of Social Sciences and a professor of law at Beijing University, answered questions raised on November 21 by reporters from Xinhua News Agency on some legal questions involved in the trial. Excerpts follow:

Q. What are the legal grounds for the Special Court of the Supreme People's Court's using the Criminal Law of the People's Republic of China in the trial of the Lin Biao and Jiang Qing counter-revolutionary cliques instead of the Regulations Governing the Punishment of Counter-Revolutionaries and other decrees in force when they committed the counter-revolutionary offences with which they are charged?

A. On the question of the application of the law, Article 9 of China's Criminal Law stipulates: "If an act performed after the founding of the People's Republic of China and prior to enforcement of the present law was not deemed an offence under the laws, decrees and policies then in force, those laws, decrees and policies shall be the standard. If the act was deemed an offence under those laws, decrees and policies and is also subject to prosecution under Section 8, Chapter 4, of the General Provisions of the present law, the standard of criminal liability shall also be those laws, decrees and policies. But, if the act is not deemed an offence or the penalty for the offence is lighter under the present law, the present law shall apply."

The defendants are charged with such crimes as subverting the government, splitting the state, engineering an armed rebellion, framing and persecuting people, having people injured or murdered and conducting demagogical propaganda for counter-revolutionary ends, extorting confessions by torture and illegally detaining people — all deemed offences under both the past laws and the present Criminal Law.

Article 9 of the Criminal Law lays down the principle of applying the new law if punishment under it is lighter than under the old ones. The past laws, decrees and policies generally provide for heavier sentence than the present Criminal Law for identical offences. For instance, almost every article of the Regulations carries the death sentence, whereas there are fewer death sentences in the articles of the chapter on counter-revolutionary crimes in the present Criminal Law.

This shows that application of the Criminal Law to the present case conforms to the principle of "lighter penalty." It not only complies with the legal principle but also has legal basis.

It should be made clear that the principle that a new law is to be applied retroactively when it carries lighter penalty than the old is not an invention of China's, but the general international practice.

Q. What is the legal basis for not having people's assessors at the trial?

A. Article 9 of the Organic Law of the People's Courts

of the People's Republic of China specifies that "the people's courts apply the system of people's assessors in all cases of first instance, with the exception of simple civil cases, minor criminal cases and cases otherwise provided for by law."

In view of the special gravity of the case of the Lin Biao and Jiang Qing counter-revolutionary cliques, the 16th session of the Fifth N.P.C. Standing Committee adopted a decision to establish a Special Court under the Supreme People's Court and appoint the president and three vice-presidents of the Special Court and 31 judges.

This decision is a decree and has legal effect. According to Article 9 of the Organic Law of the People's Courts, the case of the Lin Biao and Jiang Qing counter-revolutionary cliques is a case of last instance belonging to "the cases otherwise provided for by law," in which the system of people's assessors need not apply.

Q. Why is the number of people admitted to the hearing at the Special Court restricted? Is this peculiar to China?

A. All countries restrict the number of people attending a court session. The stipulations on trial attendance vary from country to country. Some require applications and registration while others issue certificates for attendance at a session. In this trial in China, the method used is to issue tickets for court attendance. One ticket to a person, totalling over 800 on the opening day of the trial.

Among those present in the public gallery are representatives of various provinces, autonomous regions and municipalities directly under the central government, political parties, people's organizations, state institutions and the People's Liberation Army. Since the case is especially grave and involves many important state secrets, it is normal not to issue tickets to foreigners.

Q. There are people abroad who hold that guilt was

established before the trial and that the court will do no more than determine the gravity of the punishment and thus contradict the principle of "the presumption of innocence." Would you care to comment?

A. This shows misunderstanding of the principles of China's criminal procedure. We adhere to the principle of basing ourselves on facts and taking the law as the criterion. Our trial procedure ensures the implementation of this principle. Before the end of the trial, the court will presume the accused neither guilty nor innocent, but will judge on the basis of facts during the trial.

In accordance with this principle, the Special Court will, in line with the trial procedure stipulated by the Procedural Law, pass judgement on the innocence or guilt of the accused and, if they are found guilty, determine the gravity of punishment.

Answers by Wang Hanbin

Wang Hanbin, Vice-Chairman of the Commission for Legal Affairs of the N.P.C. Standing Committee, answered questions put by Beijing Review *on behalf of its foreign readers. Excerpts follow:*

Q: Before the court's verdict is announced, some readers noted, reports and comments in the Chinese media all asserted that the defendants were guilty. Would this in some way affect the independent judgement of the court?

A: It is true that our public opinion circles generally hold that the chief offenders of the Lin Biao and Jiang Qing counter-revolutionary cliques have committed heinous crimes and don't follow some other countries' principle of "presumption of innocence."

According to China's Law of Criminal Procedure, our

trial procedure ensures the implementation of the principles of basing ourselves on facts and taking the law as the criterion. Before trial ends, the court does not presume the accused guilty or innocent, but decides on the basis of facts. It attaches importance to evidence and investigation and does not accept confessions lightly.

The Lin Biao and Jiang Qing cliques played havoc for about ten years and did great harm to the Chinese people. Though the mass media was controlled by these cliques during those years, people throughout the country still sought all sorts of ways to expose their crimes and express their own anger and hatred for them. The famous Tian An Men revolutionary incident in April 1976 well reflected this kind of feeling when tens of thousands of Beijing citizens went to Tian An Men Square to lay their poems and prose, many denouncing the Gang of Four, on funeral wreaths for Premier Zhou, on the balustrades of the Monument to the Heroes of the People and in other places of the square. Many handed out leaflets and statements listing the crimes of the Gang, braving the danger of arrest. After the Gang's downfall, the media returned to the hands of the people. How could they keep silent and not reflect the people's thinking before the court makes its decision?

However, though the comments of the press, radio and television hold that the accused are guilty before the court decides, this doesn't mean that they are legally guilty. The judgement — whether they are guilty or not, what offences they committed and what sentences should be given — has to be made by the court on the basis of facts and according to law. Public opinion does not interfere in the independent judgement of the court.

Legal systems vary in different countries. In some countries the media are not supposed to say anything before the court delivers its verdict whether a defendant is guilty or not; in other countries it is different. China's socialist legal system needs to be improved and strengthened. While enacting laws, we should take into consideration and absorb the useful parts of laws in other countries and those of our past laws. But, as regards our judicial work, we must follow our present laws, not something else.

Q: Many members of the Special Procuratorate and the Special Court were framed and persecuted by the Lin-Jiang cliques. According to stipulations in China's Law of Criminal Procedure, it seems that they should withdraw from exercising their functions. Why should they be allowed to handle the case?

A: It's true that the Law of Criminal Procedure has made stipulations about withdrawal. But the Lin Biao and Jiang Qing counter-revolutionary cliques have brought the entire country and nation unimaginable disasters and the people of the whole country suffered. Should there be a withdrawal, everyone would have to do so. That would mean only the accused themselves or their followers could try the case. This is obviously impossible.

Members of the Special Procuratorate and Special Court were all appointed by the Standing Committee of the National People's Congress and they were entrusted by the people of the whole country to prefer public charges against and conduct the trial of the principal defendants of the Lin Biao and Jiang Qing counter-revolutionary cliques. In this respect, the case differs entirely from ordinary criminal cases. In special cases like this, there is no question of withdrawal. This was also the practice during the trial of the arch war criminals of Germany and Japan in Nuremberg and Tokyo. Both courts were formed by the victorious nations and the principle of non-withdrawal and allowing no withdrawal was adopted.

Remarks by Liu Fuzhi

Liu Fuzhi, Vice-chairman of the Commission for Legal Affairs of the N.P.C. Standing Committee, spoke to some reporters from Xinhua News Agency on January 20, 1981, five days before the Special Court announced its judgement. Liu Fuzhi gave his views on the principles for meting out punishment to culprits. Excerpts of his remarks follow:

The charges against the accused fall under a number of articles of the Criminal Law. Provisions for punishment for these offences range from death penalty in serious cases to varying terms of imprisonment.*

The Criminal Law also states that counter-revolutionaries shall be deprived of political rights. An offender sentenced to life imprisonment shall be permanently deprived of political rights.

If he is sentenced to a fixed term, with deprivation of political rights as a supplementary penalty, that deprivation shall be from one to five years, starting on the day he finishes his jail term, in addition to deprivation of political rights while he is in jail.

Penalties are determined according to the relevant provisions of the Criminal Law, the nature of the offence and the degree of damage to society.

The Law provides for a range of penalties for each offence to allow the court some discretion. In cases of counter-revolutionary homicide and injury, for instance, the penalty can vary from three years to death, according to the court's discretion.

The court may also make a difference between prin-

---

* See page 130 for articles from the Criminal Law relevant to the present case.

cipal defendants and accomplices; between offenders who give themselves up and those who do not.

Where mitigating circumstances are present, such as otherwise meritorious behaviour, the court may impose a lesser penalty or remit the penalty. It cannot pass a heavier sentence than the maximum provided for under the relevant article.

Every offence has a certain limitation period and no prosecution can be instituted after that period expires. The period of limitation runs from the day of the commission of the crime. In successive or continuous offences, it runs from the last day of the offences.

It has been nine years since the surviving members of the Lin Biao clique were taken into custody in 1971. Therefore, they could not be prosecuted on charges of slander or unlawfully searching and ransacking people's homes.

On the other hand, prosecution was permitted on charges of attempting to overthrow the government, organizing and leading a counter-revolutionary clique and of framing and persecuting people.

It has been less than five years since Jiang Qing and the other members of her clique were deposed and the limitation of prosecution for unlawful search and ransacking of people's homes has not run out.

Offenders who have committed several offences may be liable to a compound penalty. The compound jail term shall not exceed the sum of the terms for the individual offences, nor be shorter than the longest individual term.

In any case, a compound jail term imposed for several offences shall not exceed 20 years.

Qiu Shaoheng's Views

Jurist, Professor Qiu Shaoheng (known abroad as Henry Chiu) spoke to reporters from Xinhua News Agency on January 29 about his impressions of the trial of the Lin-Jiang case. Qiu was secretary of the Chinese delegation to the International Military Tribunal held in Tokyo after World War II. During the trial of Jiang Qing and nine other defendants, he attended most of the court sessions. Excerpts of his comments follow:

The trial of the Lin-Jiang cliques was fair. China's new Criminal Law which became effective on January 1 last year was correctly applied to the ten defendants. The importance of investigation and evidence was upheld and all defendants were guaranteed the right to a defence.

The judges played a relatively active role in the Special Court, because under the Chinese legal system they are freer to question the parties and witnesses than are judges in countries following common law traditions, such as England and the United States.

The role of the trial judge in China is to search for facts, listen to witnesses, examine documents and make further investigations if he considers them necessary. This is similar to Continental law methods practised in some European countries and is quite different from the procedure followed in most common law countries in which prosecuting and defence attorneys play the most active role in finding and presenting evidence. The role of the Chinese judge is of course guided by legal procedure which expressly forbids the obtaining of evidence by threat, inducement, fraud or other unlawful means.

A defendant in a Chinese criminal court is presumed neither innocent nor guilty. China's Law of Criminal Procedure is designed to ensure prompt and accurate findings of fact and correct application of the law for the purpose of punishing the offenders and protecting the innocent from criminal liability.

Stress is laid on evidence and investigation, and a defendant's confession is not taken for granted. The law stipulates that a defendant cannot be convicted and sentenced on the basis of a confession if there is no corroborating evidence; but can be judged guilty and sentenced without a confession if there is sufficient evidence to establish guilt. During the trial, a majority of defendants admitted guilt but Jiang Qing disrupted order in court while Zhang Chunqiao remained silent throughout the proceedings. In these cases, there was ample evidence to convict the defendants even though they had not made confessions.

All the defendants had been given the right to defend themselves at the trial and to have defence counsel if they wished, as provided by Chinese law. Five of them did appoint defence counsel, while some decided to argue on their own behalf.

Zhang Chunqiao wanted no counsel and sat mute throughout the hearings, though he was urged many times by the presiding judge to make his own pleadings. If there was anyone who deprived him of the right to defence, it was he himself.

The trial concluded on January 25 with Jiang Qing and Zhang Chunqiao receiving death sentences with a two-year reprieve and others prison terms ranging from 16 years to life. The evidence at the trial proved that Lin Biao, Jiang Qing and their cohorts had intended to overthrow the people's democratic dictatorship through usurping supreme power. Such a plot and the sinister means the cliques employed would be equally indictable crimes in any other country. The attempted assassination of Chairman Mao Zedong and the plot for an armed rebellion in Shanghai are ready examples of flagrant crimes.

INDICTMENT

OF

THE SPECIAL PROCURATORATE UNDER
THE SUPREME PEOPLE'S PROCURATORATE OF
THE PEOPLE'S REPUBLIC OF CHINA

Te Jian Zi No. 1

To the Special Court Under the
Supreme People's Court of the
People's Republic of China:

The Ministry of Public Security of the People's Republic of China, after concluding its investigation, has referred the case of the plot of the Lin Biao and Jiang Qing counter-revolutionary cliques to overthrow the political power of the dictatorship of the proletariat to the Supreme People's Procuratorate of the People's Republic of China for examination and prosecution.

Having examined the case, the Special Procuratorate Under the Supreme People's Procuratorate confirms that the principal culprits of the Lin Biao and Jiang Qing counter-revolutionary cliques, namely, Lin Biao, Jiang Qing, Kang Sheng, Zhang Chunqiao, Yao Wenyuan, Wang Hongwen, Chen Boda, Xie Fuzhi, Ye Qun, Huang Yongsheng, Wu Faxian, Li Zuopeng, Qiu Huizuo, Lin Liguo, Zhou Yuchi and Jiang Tengjiao, acted in collusion during the "great cultural revolution" and, taking advantage of their positions and the power at their disposal, framed and persecuted Communist Party and state leaders in a premeditated way in their attempts to usurp Party leadership and state power and overthrow the political power of the dictatorship of the proletariat. They did this by resorting to all kinds of intrigues and using every possible means, legal or illegal, overt or covert, by pen or by gun. In September 1971, after the plot of Lin Biao, Ye Qun, Lin Liguo, Zhou Yuchi and Jiang Tengjiao to murder Chairman Mao Zedong and stage an armed counter-revolutionary coup d'etat failed, Lin Biao and others defected and fled the country, and the counter-revolutionary clique headed by him was exposed and crushed. The counter-revolutionary gang of four consisting of Jiang Qing, Zhang Chunqiao, Yao Wenyuan and Wang Hongwen, with Jiang Qing at the head, continued its conspiratorial counter-revolutionary activities until it was exposed and smashed in October 1976. The Lin Biao and Jiang Qing counter-revolutionary cliques brought untold disasters to our country and nation.

The Lin Biao and Jiang Qing counter-revolutionary cliques committed the following crimes:

I

Frame-Up and Persecution of Party and State Leaders and Plotting to Overthrow the Political Power of the Dictatorship of the Proletariat

To overthrow the political power of the dictatorship of the proletariat, the Lin Biao and Jiang Qing counter-revolutionary cliques framed and persecuted Party and state leaders and leading cadres in all walks of life in a premeditated way.

(1) They instigated the persecution of Party and state leaders at all levels in their attempts to seize leadership. On January 23, 1967, Lin Biao plotted the usurpation of power, saying, "All power, be it at the top, middle or lower levels, should be seized. In some cases, this should be done sooner, in others later." "This may be done at the top or lower levels, or done in co-ordination at both levels." He also instigated the persecution of leading cadres. He said, "Put some of them in custody, cap some with tall paper hats, and search and ransack the homes of others." "It is necessary to use measures such as the 'jet aircraft' (forcing a person to bow with both hands raised over his back, like the swept-back wings of a jet plane — Tr.) against people like Peng Zhen, Luo Ruiqing, Lu Dingyi and Yang Shangkun."

Zhang Chunqiao said in Shanghai on January 22, 1967, "Our aim in the Great Proletarian Cultural Revolution has always been to seize power, from the grass roots to the central organizations, including the powers of the Party and the government, as well as in the financial, cultural and other fields." "We must seize power everywhere." With regard to veteran cadres he said in Shanghai in April, "All of them are bad" and "None shall be spared!" From 1967 to 1975, he said on many other occasions in Shanghai and Beijing that "the great cultural revolution" meant "a change of dynasty." In plotting to usurp power and effect a "change of dynasty," the Lin Biao and Jiang Qing counter-revolutionary cliques laid bare their counter-revolutionary objective of overthrowing the political power of the proletarian dictatorship.

(2) They brought false charges against and persecuted Liu Shaoqi, Chairman of the People's Republic of China and Vice-Chairman of the Central Committee of the Communist Party of China (C.P.C.). In August 1966, when

Liu Shaoqi was still Chairman of the People's Republic of China (P.R.C.) and was re-elected to the Standing Committee of the Political Bureau of the C.P.C. Central Committee, Lin Biao instructed Ye Qun to summon Lei Yingfu twice to her presence, first on August 11 and then 12. Lei Yingfu was then deputy director of the Operations Department of the Headquarters of the General Staff of the Chinese People's Liberation Army (P.L.A.). She provided him verbally with material containing false charges fabricated by Lin Biao and herself against Liu Shaoqi and instructed him to put these charges in writing. On August 13, Lin Biao read what Lei had written. At his residence, Lin told Lei the next day that "it will look more political" if Lei would write an accompanying letter addressed to Lin Biao and Chairman Mao Zedong, so that Lin could write his comments on the letter before forwarding it to the Chairman. On the same day, Lin Biao sent Lei Yingfu's letter together with his material incriminating Liu Shaoqi to Jiang Qing for her to "consider forwarding" them to the Chairman.

On the afternoon of December 18, 1966, Zhang Chunqiao met privately with Kuai Dafu, a Qinghua University student, in the reception room at the west gate of Zhongnanhai, Beijing. He said, "That couple of persons in the Central Committee who put forward the reactionary bourgeois line have not yet surrendered. . . . You young revolutionary fighters should unite, carry forward your thoroughgoing revolutionary spirit and flog the cur that has fallen into the water. Make their very names stink. Don't stop half way." Incited by Zhang, Kuai organized a demonstration in Beijing on December 25. The demonstrators put up slogans and big-character posters, handed out leaflets and shouted demagogically, "Down with Liu Shaoqi!" and "Down with Deng Xiaoping!"

In July 1967, Jiang Qing, Kang Sheng and Chen Boda decided without authorization that Liu Shaoqi should be repudiated and struggled against. Qi Benyu, a member of the "Cultural Revolution Group Under the C.P.C. Central Committee," organized a "rally for repudiating and struggling against Liu Shaoqi" on July 18 of the same year; the residence of Liu Shaoqi and Wang Guangmei was searched and ransacked and the two were physically harassed. During July and August 1967, Kang Sheng, Xie Fuzhi and Qi Benyu incited people to organize a "frontline for getting Liu Shaoqi out of Zhongnanhai," surround the place and attempt to break into the State Council.

Jiang Qing assumed direct control of the "group for inquiring into the special case of Liu Shaoqi and Wang Guangmei" and directed its work in collusion with Kang Sheng and Xie Fuzhi. They rigged up false evidence by extorting confessions through torture in order to vilify Liu Shaoqi and Wang Guangmei as "renegades," "enemy agents" and "counter-revolutionaries." From May to October 1967, acting on her own, Jiang Qing took the decision to arrest and imprison Yang Yichen, Deputy Governor of Hebei Province; Yang Chengzuo, a professor at the China People's University in Beijing; Wang Guangen, a resident of Tianjin (originally assistant manager of the former Fengtian Cotton Mill); Liu Shaoqi's former cook Hao Miao; and seven others. When Yang Chengzuo became critically ill, Jiang Qing said to the group for inquiring into the special case, "Step up the interrogation to squeeze out of him what we need before he dies." Yang Chengzuo died as a result of persecution. So was Wang Guangen. On October 23, 1967, Xie Fuzhi said to the special case group, "It is necessary to be firm and ruthless in interrogation. . . . It is necessary to carry out group interrogation for hours at a time until confessions are obtained." In order to frame Wang Guangmei as an "enemy agent," Jiang Qing and Xie Fuzhi ordered the interrogation and torture of Zhang Zhongyi, a professor at the Hebei Provincial Normal College in Beijing who was critically ill. Zhang was tortured to death. In order to frame Liu Shaoqi as a "renegade," they extorted confessions from Ding Juequn, who worked with Liu Shaoqi in the workers' movement in Wuhan in 1927, and Meng Yongqian, who was arrested with Liu Shaoqi in Shenyang in 1929. On September 25, 1967, Ding declared in prison that the confession he was compelled to write "does not strictly conform to facts." Between June 15, 1967 and March 18, 1969, Meng wrote 20 statements in prison declaring that what he had written about Liu Shaoqi under duress "was mere fabrication" and should be withdrawn. But all their requests to make corrections to their statements and all their appeals were withheld and not allowed to be submitted to higher authorities. Liu Shaoqi died as a result of persecution.

(3) Jiang Qing and Kang Sheng cooked up false charges to persecute Members of the Eighth Central Committee of the C.P.C. On July 21, 1968, Kang Sheng wrote a strictly confidential letter. On the envelope he wrote "Important. To be forwarded immediately to and personally opened by Comrade Jiang Qing." In the letter, he wrote, "Enclosed please find the name list you have asked for." On this list drawn up by Kang Sheng in his own handwriting, 88 of the 193 Members and Alternate Members of the Eighth Central Committee of the C.P.C. were falsely charged as "enemy agents," "renegades," "elements having illicit relations with foreign countries" or "anti-Party elements." Another seven were classified as having been temporarily "removed from their posts but not yet included among the special cases" and 29 were classified as "having made mistakes or needing to be subjected to investigation for their historical records." Later, the great majority of them were also framed and persecuted by Kang Sheng and others.

Among the Party and state leaders and the first secretaries of the regional bureaus of the Central Committee of the Communist Party who were thus framed were:

Members and Alternate Members of the Political Bureau of the Central Committee of the C.P.C.: Liu Shaoqi, Zhu De, Chen Yun, Deng Xiaoping, Peng Zhen, Chen Yi, Peng Dehuai, He Long, Li Xiannian, Tan Zhenlin, Li Jingquan, Tao Zhu, Xu Xiangqian, Nie Rongzhen, Ye Jianying, Ulanhu, Zhang Wentian, Lu Dingyi, Bo Yibo and Song Renqiong.

General Secretary of the Central Committee of the C.P.C. Deng Xiaoping; Members and Alternate Members of the Secretariat of the Central Committee of the C.P.C.: Peng Zhen, Wang Jiaxiang, Tan Zhenlin, Li Xiannian, Lu Dingyi, Luo Ruiqing, Tao Zhu, Ye Jianying, Liu Ningyi, Liu Lantao, Yang Shangkun and Hu Qiaomu.

Vice-Premiers of the State Council: Chen Yun, Deng Xiaoping, He Long, Chen Yi, Ulanhu, Li Xiannian, Tan Zhenlin, Nie Rongzhen, Bo Yibo, Lu Dingyi, Luo Ruiqing and Tao Zhu.

Vice-Chairmen of the Military Commission of the Central Committee of the C.P.C.: He Long, Nie Rongzhen, Chen Yi, Xu Xiangqian and Ye Jianying.

First secretaries of the regional bureaus of the Central Committee of the C.P.C.: Song Renqiong, Liu Lantao, Li Jingquan and Wang Renzhong.

Other Members and Alternate Members of the Central Committee of the C.P.C.: Xiao Jingguang, Su Yu, Xiao Ke, Chen Shaomin, Wang Zhen, Zeng Shan, Ouyang Qin, Wang Shusheng, Wang Enmao, Deng Hua, Deng Zihui, Tan Zheng, Liu Xiao, Li Weihan, Yang Xiufeng, Zhang Jichun, Cheng Zihua, Wu Xiuquan, Qian Ying, Wang Congwu, Ma Mingfang, Li Baohua, Xu Guangda, Lin Tie, Zheng Weisan, Xu Haidong, Xiao Hua, Hu Yaobang, Xi Zhongxun, An Ziwen, Lu Zhengcao, Zhang Jingwu, Liao Chengzhi, Ye Fei, Yang Xianzhen, Zhang Dingcheng, Shu

Tong, Pan Zili, Yang Yong, Huang Huoqing, Chen Man-
yuan, Su Zhenhua, Feng Baiju, Fan Wenlan, Li Jianzhen,
Gao Kelin, Zhong Qiguang, Jiang Hua, Li Zhimin, Yang
Chengwu, Zhang Hanfu, Shuai Mengqi, Liu Ren, Wan Yi,
Zhou Yang, Xu Zirong, Liu Lanbo, Kui Bi, Ou Mengjue,
Zhu Dehai, Zhang Qilong, Ma Wenrui, Wang Shitai, Liao
Hansheng, Hong Xuezhi, Zhang Yun, Xu Bing, Liao Lu-
yan, Song Shilun, Zhou Huan, Chen Pixian, Zhao Jian-
min, Qian Junrui, Jiang Nanxiang, Han Guang, Li Chang,
Wang Heshou, Chen Zhengren, Zhao Yimin, Kong Yuan,
Zhang Su, Yang Yichen, Zhao Boping, Zhang Aiping, Yao
Yilin, Wang Feng, Fang Yi, Wang Shangrong, Liu Zhen,
Zhang Jingfu, Li Jiebo, Liao Zhigao, Jiang Weiqing, Tan
Qilong, Zhang Zhongliang and Zhang Pinghua.

(4) Chen Boda, Xie Fuzhi and Wu Faxian made use of
the case of the so-called "Extraordinary Central Committee of the Communist Party of China" leaflet, which
had been uncovered in Tianjin in November 1967, to
frame and persecute Party and state leaders under the
pretext of tracking down the "behind-the-scenes bosses."
On April 28 and August 19, 1968, when they received
Zhao Dengcheng, then a member of the leading group at
the Ministry of Public Security, and others, Chen Boda
said that the uncovering of the case was merely "the beginning." He added, "It is not the end. The bosses are
hidden behind the scenes, and they are no ordinary persons, for ordinary people aren't capable of doing such a
thing. It isn't the act of one individual. Very likely,
there's an organization behind all this." Xie Fuzhi cut in
saying, "Yes, it's merely the beginning, not the end."
He added, "Somebody from the notorious Liu-Deng headquarters is at the root of it all." Wu Faxian said, "Who
else can it be but Capitalist Roader No. 2?" In December
1968, while tracking down the "behind-the-scenes bosses,"
Xie Fuzhi, Zhao Dengcheng and others cooked up the
false case of a "Chinese Communist Party (M-L)," with

Zhu De as the alleged "secretary" of its central committee, Chen Yi as "deputy secretary and concurrently minister of defence," and Li Fuchun as "premier." Its members allegedly included Dong Biwu, Ye Jianying, Li Xiannian, He Long, Liu Bocheng, Xu Xiangqian, Nie Rongzhen, Tan Zhenlin, Yu Qiuli, Wang Zhen and Liao Chengzhi, who were falsely accused of having "illicit relations with foreign countries," "making preparations for an armed insurrection" and attempting to "stage a coup." Even up to August 21, 1969, Xie Fuzhi told those who were responsible for inquiring into the case, "Be firm and keep up your inquiries, for some evidence is still lacking. The verbal confessions made by those jailed can be used as evidence, too."

(5) Kang Sheng and his wife Cao Yiou instructed Guo Yufeng, who was in charge of the Organization Department of the C.P.C. Central Committee, to provide on August 23, 1968 a fabricated "Report on the Political Background of Members of the Control Commission of the Central Committee of the C.P.C." In the report, 37 of the 60 Members and Alternate Members of the Control Commission of the Eighth Central Committee of the C.P.C. were falsely labelled "renegades," "enemy agents" or "counter-revolutionary revisionists." They were: Liu Lantao, Wang Congwu, Qian Ying, Liu Xiwu, Shuai Mengqi, Li Yunchang, Wang Weigang, Yang Zhihua, Li Shiying, Li Chuli, Ma Mingfang, Gong Zirong, Chen Shaomin, Fang Zhongru, Liu Yaxiong, Zhang Ziyi, Wang Hefeng, Liu Shenzhi, Li Peizhi, Zhou Zhongying, Chen Peng, Chen Zenggu, Zheng Ping, Xue Zizheng, Gao Kelin, Ji Yatai, Wang Shiying, Qiu Jin, Wu Gaizhi, Ma Guorui, Zhang Dingcheng, Wu Defeng, Zhang Jiafu, Liao Suhua, Gong Fengchun, Li Jingying and Xiao Hua.

(6) Kang Sheng and Cao Yiou instructed Guo Yufeng to fabricate on August 27, 1968 a "Report on the Political Background of Members of the Standing Committee of

the Third National People's Congress," which was subsequently revised and finalized by Kang Sheng himself. In the report, 60 of the 115 Members were framed as "renegades," "suspected renegades," "enemy agents," "suspected enemy agents," "counter-revolutionary revisionists, capitalist roaders or anti-Party, anti-socialist and anti-Mao Zedong Thought elements" and "highly dubious characters." They were: Chairman of the Standing Committee Zhu De; Vice-Chairmen Peng Zhen, Li Jingquan, Lin Feng, Liu Ningyi and Zhang Zhizhong; and Members Chen Shaomin, Yang Zhihua, Shuai Mengqi, Zhao Yimin, Qian Ying, Liu Yaxiong, Li Da, Xu Liqing, Wang Shitai, Hu Ziang, Liu Lanbo, Xu Bing, Xu Zirong, Zhang Jingwu, Yang Shangkun, Li Yanlu, Han Guang, Mei Gongbin, Wang Kunlun, Nan Hanchen, Gong Yinbing, Cao Mengjun, Shi Liang, Tang Shengzhi, Kong Yuan, Hu Yaobang, Xie Fumin, Luo Qiong, Wu Lengxi, Zhang Su, Wu Xinyu, Ma Chungu, Yu Aifeng, Liu Changsheng, Gu Dacun, Zhou Li, Zhao Shoushan, Hu Yuzhi, Hu Qiaomu, Liang Sicheng, Tong Dizhou, Ye Zhupei, Chen Qiyou, Wang Weizhou, Ye Jianying, Lin Qiangyun, Guo Jian, Yang Yunyu, Hua Luogeng, Zhao Zhongyao, Chen Shaoxian, Zhao Jiuzhang, Mao Yisheng and Hu Juewen.

(7) Kang Sheng and Cao Yiou instructed Guo Yufeng to fabricate on August 27, 1968 a "Report on the Political Background of Members of the Standing Committee of the Fourth National Committee of the Chinese People's Political Consultative Conference," which was subsequently revised and finalized by Kang Sheng himself. In the report, 74 of the 159 Members were falsely accused of being "renegades," "suspected renegades," "enemy agents," "suspected enemy agents," "Kuomintang agents," "counter-revolutionary revisionists," or "having illicit relations with foreign countries." They were: Vice-Chairmen Peng Zhen, Liu Lantao, Song Renqiong, Xu Bing and Gao Chongmin; and Members Wang Congwu,

Liu Xiwu, Ping Jiesan, Yang Dongchun, Li Chuli, Wang Weigang, Zhang Ziyi, Li Yunchang, Gong Zirong, Li Chulee, Cao Ying, Liu Qingyang, Kong Xiangzhen, Ma Huizhi, Zhang Youyu, Zhang Yun, Wang Zhaohua, Zhou Yang, Wu Gaizhi, He Changgong, Lin Xiude, Tang Tianji, Zhu Yunshan, Su Ziheng, Gong Tianmin, Zou Dapeng, An Ziwen, Chu Tunan, Wang Jinxiang, Li Lisan, Zeng Xianzhi, Sa Kongliao, Zhang Xiuyan, Ji Yatai, Yu Yifu, Ha Fenga, Wang Shiying, Liu Xiao, Yan Baohang, Yang Qiqing, Sun Qimeng, Zhao Puchu, Che Xiangchen, Bainqen Erdini Qoigyi Gyaincain, Wang Jiaxiang, Wu Xiuquan, Zhang Zhizhong, Sun Xiaocun, Shi Liang, Chu Xuefan, Liu Fei, Zhang Xiaoqian, Cun Shusheng, Yu Dafu, Zheng Weisan, Chen Guodong, Gao Wenhua, Wang Zigang, Zhang Bangying, Hu Keshi, Li Chang, He Cheng, Zhong Huilan, Wu Hongbin, Fu Lianzhang, Jin Rubai, Chen Qiyou, Xiong Qinglai and Zhang Jingfu.

(8)   The frame-up and persecution of Zhou Enlai, Vice-Chairman of the Central Committee of the C.P.C. and Premier of the State Council.   In October 1974, Jiang Qing falsely accused Zhou Enlai and others of conspiracy, saying, "Those people in the State Council often maintain illicit contact with each other on the pretext of discussing work. . . .   The Premier is the boss behind the scenes." On October 17, 1974, the gang of four, namely, Jiang Qing, Zhang Chunqiao, Yao Wenyuan and Wang Hongwen, hatched a plot in Building No. 17 at Diao Yu Tai in Beijing and the following day sent Wang Hongwen to Changsha to make a false and insinuating report to Chairman Mao Zedong.   He said, "Although the Premier is ill and hospitalized, he is busy summoning people for talks far into the night.   Almost every day someone visits him. Deng Xiaoping, Ye Jianying and Li Xiannian are frequent visitors."   He added, "The atmosphere in Beijing now is very much like that at the Lushan Meeting."   He was falsely accusing Zhou Enlai, Deng Xiaoping and others

of engaging in activities to usurp power as Lin Biao had during the Lushan Meeting in 1970. In 1974, Jiang Qing, Zhang Chunqiao and Yao Wenyuan instructed Chi Qun, then secretary of the C.P.C. Committee of Qinghua University, Xie Jingyi, then secretary of the Beijing Municipal Committee of the C.P.C., Lu Ying, editor-in-chief of *Renmin Ribao* (*People's Daily*), Zhu Yongjia, then head of the Shanghai Writing Group, and others to make use of the media to stir up nationwide criticism of the "big Confucian of our time," the "chief minister" and the "Duke of Zhou," thus attacking Zhou Enlai by innuendo.

(9) The frame-up and persecution of Zhu De, Vice-Chairman of the Central Committee of the C.P.C. and Chairman of the Standing Committee of the National People's Congress. From September 1966 to December 1968, Lin Biao, Zhang Chunqiao, Wu Faxian, Qiu Huizuo and others slandered Zhu De and falsely accused him of being a "sinister commander," an "old-line opportunist" and a "warlord" and of "harbouring wild ambitions to become the leader."

At the end of January 1967, at the instigation of Qi Benyu, some people from the China People's University put up large-size slogans in Beijing, which read "Down with Zhu De." Presently the "Liaison Centre for Ferreting Out Zhu De" was set up and a plot was under way to hold meetings to repudiate him. On March 4, Qi Benyu received people from the China People's University and incited them to continue with their persecution of Zhu De. He said, "If you do it yourselves, you will succeed. But if you tell people that I'm behind all this, you won't succeed. You think you're smart. Actually you're a bunch of fatheads. It's up to you to decide whether you go on or not."

(10) The frame-up and persecution of Deng Xiaoping, Member of the Standing Committee of the Political

Bureau of the Central Committee of the C.P.C., General Secretary of the Central Committee and Vice-Premier of the State Council. On December 6, 1966, Lin Biao slandered Deng Xiaoping as a "member of a sinister gang" and as an "anti-Party element." And on January 29, 1967, Kang Sheng vilified Deng Xiaoping, as a "Khrushchov-type person."

On October 4, 1974, Chairman Mao Zedong proposed that Deng Xiaoping be First Vice-Premier of the State Council. In an attempt to prevent Deng Xiaoping from taking office, Jiang Qing, Zhang Chunqiao, Yao Wenyuan and Wang Hongwen conspired together on October 17 in Building No. 17 at Diao Yu Tai in Beijing and had Wang Hongwen go to Changsha the following day to report to Chairman Mao Zedong with the false charge that Zhou Enlai, Deng Xiaoping and others were engaged in activities to seize power.

From February to May 1976, Jiang Qing, Zhang Chunqiao, Yao Wenyuan and Mao Yuanxin, another key member of the Jiang Qing counter-revolutionary clique, went a step further in their false accusations against Deng Xiaoping. Document No. 1 of the Central Committee of the C.P.C. of 1975 had carried the appointment of Deng Xiaoping as Vice-Chairman of the Military Commission of the C.P.C. Central Committee and concurrently Chief of the General Staff of the P.L.A. and Document No. 1 of the Central Committee of the C.P.C. of 1976 had carried the appointment of Hua Guofeng as Acting Premier of the State Council. Regarding these two documents, Zhang Chunqiao wrote on February 3, 1976, "Here is yet another Document No. 1. There was a Document No. 1 last year. This is truly a case of inflated arrogance at an upturn in fortune. Moving up so fast and so hurriedly spells a downfall that will be just as rapid." and he quoted a classical poem:

161

A year ends amidst the crepitation of firecrackers,
An easterly breeze has warmed the New Year's
wine.
The doors of every household are bathed in the
sunshine,
A new peach-wood lintel charm invariably replaces
the old.

This again revealed Zhang Chunqiao's counter-revolutionary ambition to effect a "change of dynasty." On February 22, Mao Yuanxin said to Ma Tianshui and Xu Jingxian, then vice-chairmen of the Shanghai Municipal Revolutionary Committee, and others that Deng Xiaoping "worships things foreign and sells out the sovereignty of the country" and that he "represents the interests of the comprador bourgeoisie" and was trying to bring about an "all-round retrogression" so that "there would be a change in the nature of the state." On March 2, at a forum of leading members from a number of provinces and autonomous regions, Jiang Qing maligned Deng Xiaoping, calling him a "counter-revolutionary double-dealer," the "general manager of a rumour-mongering company," a "fascist," a "big quisling" and a "representative of the comprador bourgeoisie." On April 26, Jiang Qing falsely charged that Deng Xiaoping, like Lin Biao, had "big and small fleets" (gangs formed to carry out plots and assassinations — *Tr.*) and that "their fleets operated in about the same way in some cases, and differently in others. Deng's small fleets are, however, more active." On April 5, Zhang Chunqiao slanderously accused Deng Xiaoping of being a "Nagy." On May 16, in an article entitled "There Is Really a Bourgeoisie Within the Party — Analysis of the Counter-Revolutionary Political Incident at Tian An Men Square," which *Renmin Ribao* (*People's Daily*) sent him for finalization, Yao Wenyuan added that Deng Xiaoping "is the chief boss behind this counter-revolutionary political incident."

(11) The frame-up and persecution of Chen Yi, Member of the Political Bureau of the Central Committee of the C.P.C., Vice-Premier of the State Council and Vice-Chairman of the Military Commission of the C.P.C. Central Committee. On August 7, 1967, Wang Li, a member of the "Cultural Revolution Group Under the C.P.C. Central Committee," said, "Picking on Chen Yi is of course correct in orientation." He added, "What's wrong with the slogan 'Down with Liu (Shaoqi), Deng (Xiaoping) and Chen (Yi)?'" He was agitating people to usurp leadership over foreign affairs. In November 1968, upon Zhang Chunqiao's instruction, Wang Hongwen, Xu Jingxian and others compiled a *Collection of Chen Yi's Reactionary Views and Utterances* while nominally preparing documents for the forthcoming C.P.C. Ninth National Congress. This fabricated *Collection* was distributed in the study class of deputies from Shanghai to the Ninth National Party Congress, falsely accusing Chen Yi of "capitulating to imperialism, revisionism and reaction" and "whipping up public opinion for restoring capitalism." At the same time, they collected and compiled another 76 copies of material, running to a total of 1,163 pages, which carried false charges against Ye Jianying, Li Xiannian, Chen Yun, Chen Yi, Nie Rongzhen, Li Fuchun, Tan Zhenlin and others.

(12) The frame-up and persecution of Peng Dehuai, Member of the Political Bureau of the Central Committee of the C.P.C. In July 1967, when Kang Sheng, Chen Boda and Qi Benyu received Han Aijing and other students of the Beijing Aeronautical Engineering Institute, Qi Benyu made arrangements with them for the repudiation and persecution of Peng Dehuai. On November 3, 1970, Huang Yongsheng examined and approved a report prepared by the special case group, which

contained the proposal that "Peng Dehuai be dismissed from all posts inside and outside the Party, expelled from the Party for good, sentenced to life imprisonment and deprived of civil rights for life." Peng Dehuai died as a result of persecution.

(13) The frame-up and persecution of He Long, Member of the Political Bureau of the C.P.C. Central Committee, Vice-Premier of the State Council and Vice-Chairman of the Military Commission of the Central Committee of the C.P.C. In the summer of 1966, at a students' rally at the Beijing Normal University and at meetings of the "Cultural Revolution Group Under the C.P.C. Central Committee," Kang Sheng falsely charged He Long and Peng Zhen with "secretly deploying troops to stage a February mutiny." In August 1966, Lin Biao instructed Wu Faxian to fabricate material accusing He Long of plotting to usurp leadership in the Air Force. On September 3, Wu Faxian sent Lin Biao the material he had prepared. Between late August and early September, Ye Qun spoke to Song Zhiguo, then chief of the Guards Division of the General Office of the Military Commission of the Central Committee of the C.P.C., informing him of what she had fabricated in order to frame He Long. Then she directed him to put the material in writing, saying, "Make it sound as if you yourself were giving me the information, and not as if I had directed you to do so." From September 7 to 24 Song Zhiguo sent Lin Biao four collections of material he had prepared for framing He Long. On May 16, 1968, Kang Sheng went a step further in maligning He Long, saying, "Judging He Long's present behaviour in the light of his betrayal of the revolution and surrender to the enemy in the past, it is inconceivable that he is not now engaged in active counter-revolutionary activities. The past provides the clue to the present." He Long died as a result of persecution.

(14)   The frame-up and persecution of Xu Xiangqian, Member of the Political Bureau of the Central Committee of the C.P.C. and Vice-Chairman of its Military Commission.   In April 1967, at Ye Qun's instigation Kuai Dafu sent people to collect material for framing Xu Xiangqian and Ye Jianying and published a slanderous article entitled "Bombard Xu Xiangqian — Down with Xu Xiangqian, the Military Counterpart of Liu (Shaoqi) and Deng (Xiaoping)."   In June that year, Qiu Huizuo instructed Wang Xike, then director of the "cultural revolution office" of the P.L.A. General Logistics Department, and others to concoct material vilifying Xu Xiangqian and to edit and print leaflets slandering him as a "big time-bomb" planted in the Party and army and a "typical careerist and conspirator" and putting forward the slogan "Down with Xu Xiangqian."

(15)   The frame-up and persecution of Nie Rongzhen, Member of the Political Bureau of the Central Committee of the C.P.C., Vice-Premier of the State Council, and Vice-Chairman of the Military Commission of the Central Committee of the C.P.C.   In April 1968, Lin Biao ordered the Beijing Units of the P.L.A. to convene an enlarged Party committee meeting so as to engineer the repudiation of what they called the "mountain-stronghold mentality of north China."   He then sent Huang Yongsheng, Wu Faxian and Xie Fuzhi to the meeting.   Jiang Qing and Chen Boda falsely charged Nie Rongzhen with being the boss behind those with the "mountain-stronghold mentality of north China" and plotted to overthrow him.   In November of the same year, Huang Yongsheng slandered Nie Rongzhen, saying that "he has never done anything good all his life" and that "these people will never give up. Whenever the climate is right, they're up to something."   On January 5, 1971, Jiang Qing slandered Nie Rongzhen and others, saying

that they had been "bad people in the saddle" in north China.

(16) The frame-up and persecution of Ye Jianying, Member of the Political Bureau and of the Secretariat of the Central Committee of the C.P.C. and Vice-Chairman of its Military Commission. On June 23, 1967, Huang Yongsheng approved the "Plan on Investigation for Rounding Up Renegades," submitted by the head of the military control commission stationed in the Guangzhou Municipal Public Security Bureau, and its appendix, "Plan for Investigation, No. 1," which was directed against Ye Jianying, whom they were plotting to persecute. In June 1968, making use of the false charges he concocted in Guangzhou against Deputy Commander Wen Niansheng and others in the Guangzhou Units of the P.L.A., Huang Yongsheng launched an investigation concerning the so-called "sinister line." He later submitted to Ye Qun confessions which had been extorted, charging Ye Jianying and others with having called "secret meetings" and with "trying to usurp Party and state leadership by plotting a counter-revolutionary coup."

On April 3, 1968, Li Zuopeng, together with Wang Hongkun, then second political commissar of the Navy, and Zhang Xiuchuan, then director of the Navy's Political Department, wrote material in which they trumped up charges alleging that "He (Long) and Ye (Jianying) attempted to seize command of the armed forces to oppose the Party" in co-ordination with Liu (Shaoqi), Deng (Xiaoping) and Tao (Zhu).

(17) The frame-up and persecution of Lu Dingyi, Alternate Member of the Political Bureau of the Central Committee of the C.P.C. and Member of its Secretariat, Vice-Premier of the State Council and Director of the Propaganda Department of the C.P.C. Central Committee. In May 1966, Lin Biao trumped up charges against

Lu Dingyi, labelling him a "counter-revolutionary." Jiang Qing, Kang Sheng, Chen Boda, Xie Fuzhi, Wu Faxian and others slandered him as a "renegade," "hidden traitor" and "special agent of the Bureau of Investigation and Statistics of the Kuomintang Government's Military Council." Chen Boda said that Lu Dingyi should be "handed over to the Red Guards for trial." At the instigation and under the direction of the Lin Biao and Jiang Qing counter-revolutionary cliques, nine deputy directors of the Propaganda Department of the C.P.C. Central Committee were slandered as "renegades," "enemy agents" or "Kuomintang elements."

(18) The frame-up and persecution of Luo Ruiqing, Member of the Secretariat of the Central Committee of the C.P.C., Vice-Premier of the State Council and Chief of the General Staff of the P.L.A. Lin Biao, Ye Qun, Kang Sheng, Xie Fuzhi, Huang Yongsheng, Wu Faxian, Li Zuopeng and others trumped up charges against him, alleging that he had "illicit relations with foreign countries," was a "hidden traitor" and a "counter-revolutionary who has committed heinous crimes" and "hatched a major plot" against the Navy.

(19) Besides those people mentioned in Items (3), (4), (5), (6) and (7), others who were framed and persecuted by the Lin Biao and Jiang Qing counter-revolutionary cliques and the principal members of their factional setups include the following leading members of departments under the Central Committee of the C.P.C., ministries and commissions under the State Council, and C.P.C. committees and people's governments in provinces, autonomous regions and municipalities directly under the Central Government, and high-ranking P.L.A. cadres: Kang Keqing, Jia Tuofu, Zhou Rongxin, Gu Mu, Lu Dong, Gao Yang, Duan Junyi, Liu Jie, Sun Zhiyuan, Wang Zheng, Zhang Linzhi, Liu Yumin, Sun Daguang, Yuan Baohua, He Wei, Qian Xinzhong, Xiao

Wangdong, Wan Xiaotang, Zhang Huaisan, Zhao Lin, Zhao Ziyang, Wu Zhipu, Yan Hongyan, Wei Wenbo, Zeng Xisheng, Hui Yuyu, Wang Yanchun, Fang Zhichun, Wen Minsheng, Wei Heng, Huo Shilian, Yang Zhilin, Wang Zhao, Yang Jingren, Fu Qiutao, Liu Shaowen, Liang Biye, Liu Zhijian, Li Jukui, Rao Zhengxi, Li Yao, Peng Jiaqing, Tang Ping, Zhao Erlu, Xiao Xiangrong, Wang Ping, Cai Shunli, Liu Daosheng, Du Yide, Tao Yong, Fang Zhengping, Cheng Jun, Xu Shenji, Zhang Tingfa, Nie Fengzhi, Wu Fushan, Wu Kehua, Ouyang Yi, Liu He, He Jinnian, Cheng Shicai, Dun Xingyun, Tan Youlin, Cui Tianmin, Fu Chongbi, Zhuang Tian, Yan Fusheng, Chen Zaidao, Zhong Hanhua, Yang Xiushan, Tang Jinlong, Liu Peishan, Liu Zhuanlian, Zhang Zhonghan, Huang Xinting, Guo Linxiang, Gan Weihan, Yuan Shengping, Yang Jiarui, Qin Jiwei, Hu Ronggui, Kong Fei, Ting Mao and Wang Qimei.

(20) The frame-up and persecution of leading cadres of the Organization Department of the Central Committee of the C.P.C. and the usurpation and control of the vital organizational power of the Central Committee of the Party. In January 1968, Kang Sheng ordered Guo Yufeng to produce charts and reports to frame up charges against Zhang Wentian, Chen Yun, Peng Zhen, Deng Xiaoping and An Ziwen, who had successively served as director of the Organization Department of the Central Committee of the C.P.C. since 1937. They were falsely accused of being "renegades," "enemy agents," "elements who oppose the Party, socialism and Mao Zedong Thought," or "any combination of these." Twenty-two people, who had at one time or another served as deputy directors of the Organization Department, were falsely charged with being "renegades," "enemy agents," "elements maintaining illicit relations with foreign countries," or "elements who oppose the Party, socialism and Mao Zedong Thought." It was also

alleged that a "counter-revolutionary clique" had entrenched itself in the Organization Department, which had become "a sinister den" and had "established a nationwide network of counter-revolution which recruited renegades to form a clique to pursue its own selfish interests." And it was proposed that the Organization Department "be disbanded and abolished."

(21) The frame-up and persecution of leading cadres of the public security organs, the procuratorial organs and the courts at various levels, and the usurpation and control of the instruments of the dictatorship of the proletariat. At the instigation and under the direction of the Lin Biao and Jiang Qing counter-revolutionary cliques, the nation's public security, procuratorial and judicial organs were completely destroyed. Xie Fuzhi incited people to "smash the public security, procuratorial and judicial organs" all over the country. Zhang Dingcheng, Chief Procurator of the Supreme People's Procuratorate, Yang Xiufeng, President of the Supreme People's Court, and large numbers of cadres and policemen working in the public security organs, the procuratorial organs and the courts at various levels were framed and persecuted. Kang Sheng, Xie Fuzhi and others concocted false charges against the Ministry of Public Security, alleging that there was a so-called "underground sinister ministry of public security headed by Luo Ruiqing." With the exception of Xie Fuzhi himself and one vice-minister who held other posts concurrently, all the vice-ministers of the then Ministry of Public Security were arrested and imprisoned. Vice-Minister Xu Zirong died as a result of persecution.

(22) In January 1967, Lin Biao personally attached the comment, "I fully approve," to the slogan put forward by Guan Feng, Wang Li and other members of the "Cultural Revolution Group Under the Central Committee of the C.P.C.," that is, "Thoroughly expose the

handful of capitalist roaders in power in the People's Liberation Army." They plotted to plunge the armed forces into chaos.

In order to control the armed forces, Lin Biao fabricated charges against large numbers of cadres and masses in the Headquarters of the P.L.A. General Staff and framed and persecuted them. In April 1968, Huang Yongsheng said at the Headquarters of the General Staff, "Quite a few bad people have surfaced here, people such as Huang Kecheng, Luo Ruiqing, Zhang Aiping and Wang Shangrong," and "the verdicts against them can never be reversed; they must never be allowed to stage a comeback."

On July 25, 1967, Lin Biao called for the "thorough smashing of that Palace of Hell — the General Political Department of the People's Liberation Army." On many occasions Lin Biao and Ye Qun slandered Luo Ronghuan and Tan Zheng, former directors of the General Political Department. They trumped up charges, alleging that there was a "Luo (Ruiqing) — Liang (Biye) anti-Party clique." Huang Yongsheng vilified the General Political Department, saying that it "has been recruiting renegades under a succession of several directors." Qiu Huizuo also slandered it, saying that it was "not very different from the Kuomintang secret service." He took an active part in conspiratorial activities to "thoroughly smash the General Political Department." Large numbers of cadres and masses in the department were framed and persecuted. Four comrades who had been director or deputy director and another 20 who had been section chiefs and deputy chiefs were imprisoned and investigated under the false charge of attempting to "usurp leadership over the Army and oppose the Party" and of being "renegades," "enemy agents" or "active counter-revolutionaries." Yuan Zi-qin, Wang Bing and 15 other persons died as a result of persecution.

On March 5, 1974, Jiang Qing and Zhang Chunqiao received Chen Yading, former deputy head of the cultural section of the P.L.A. General Political Department, and others. Jiang Qing said, "Chen Yading, we have invited you here today in order to straighten things out in the Army." She added, "It seems that we have to seize power. Chen Yading, why don't you go and do it? In my opinion, we might as well let Chen Yading take charge of the Army's cultural work." She said to him and others, "You should kindle a prairie fire," thus inciting them to grab power in the Army by throwing it into disorder.

(23) Through Chen Boda and Yao Wenyuan, the Lin Biao and Jiang Qing counter-revolutionary cliques controlled the mass media and instigated the overthrow of the political power of the dictatorship of the proletariat. In June 1966, Chen Boda organized people to write, and cleared such editorials as "Sweep Away All the Monsters and Demons," thus trying to shape counter-revolutionary public opinion so that the Lin Biao and Jiang Qing counter-revolutionary cliques might usurp power after throwing the whole country into chaos. From 1974 to 1976, Jiang Qing, Zhang Chunqiao and Yao Wenyuan instructed the "Liang Xiao" writing group of Qinghua and Beijing Universities, the "Luo Siding" writing group in Shanghai, the "Chi Heng" writing group of the magazine *Hongqi* (*Red Flag*), and the "Tang Xiaowen" writing group of the Higher Party School of the Central Committee of the C.P.C. to spread counter-revolutionary, demagogic propaganda. In the spring of 1976, Yao Wenyuan personally revised and cleared such articles as "From Bourgeois Democrats to Capitalist Roaders" published in *Hongqi* (*Red Flag*) and *Renmin Ribao* (*People's Daily*). He and Zhang Chunqiao also cleared

speeches prepared for Ma Tianshui and Xu Jingxian. In these articles and speeches, they vilified veteran cadres in leading organs of the Party, government and army at various levels as "bourgeois democrats," "capitalist roaders" or "long-time capitalist roaders" and incited further persecution of them.

At the end of March 1976, slogans written in bold characters opposing Zhang Chunqiao appeared in Nanjing. Yao Wenyuan slandered the people who had put up the slogans, calling them "counter-revolutionaries." He said to Lu Ying, "It seems there's a command office stirring up this adverse, counter-revolutionary current." He added, "The situation in Beijing merits attention." Prompted by Yao Wenyuan, Lu Ying dispatched people to Tian An Men Square to collect and compile material which was then adulterated by Yao Wenyuan. Thus the revolutionary words and deeds of the masses opposing the gang of four, commemorating Zhou Enlai and supporting Deng Xiaoping were made out to be "counter-revolutionary speeches and slogans" and a "manifestation of last-ditch struggle and frenzied counterattack by the declining, moribund forces." The masses themselves were vilified as "a handful of bad elements" and "counter-revolutionaries." Yao Wenyuan even called for the "execution of a bunch of them."

From January to September 1976, at the instigation of Yao Wenyuan and Wang Hongwen, Lu Ying dispatched people to certain departments of the Party and the Government as well as to Fujian, Jiangxi, Zhejiang, Jiangsu, Sichuan, Yunnan, Heilongjiang and other provinces. There they collected material which they distorted in order to frame leading cadres in the Party, government and army, calling them "unrepentant capitalist roaders" or "capitalist roaders still travelling the capitalist road," and accusing them of "having organized landlords' restitution corps" and "trying to reverse correct verdicts and stage a comeback."

II

The Persecution and Suppression of Large Numbers of Cadres and Masses

In order to seize Party and state leadership and establish their counter-revolutionary rule, the Lin Biao and Jiang Qing counter-revolutionary cliques incited beating, smashing and looting, whipped up violence, and trumped up false charges, thus persecuting and suppressing large numbers of cadres and people.

(24) At the instigation and under the direction of Lin Biao, Jiang Qing, Kang Sheng and Xie Fuzhi, seven secretaries of the Beijing Municipal Committee of the C.P.C., including Liu Ren, Zheng Tianxiang, Wan Li and Deng Tuo, and six deputy mayors, including Wu Han and Yue Songsheng, were charged with being "enemy agents," "renegades," "counter-revolutionary revisionists," "reactionary capitalists" or "reactionary academic authorities." In January 1968, Kang Sheng falsely charged Liu Ren and deputy mayors Feng Jiping, Cui Yueli and others with "selling out vital secrets of the Party, government and army and betraying the Party and the nation." And he gave instructions to the effect that "the ordinary methods of dealing with criminals cannot be used in their case," and that "we should put them in handcuffs and carry out sudden, gruelling interrogations." In May of the same year, Kang Sheng and Xie Fuzhi concocted the case of a "counter-revolutionary clique within the former Beijing Municipal Public Security Bureau, headed by Feng Jiping and Xing Xiangsheng," falsely accusing Feng

Jiping and others of "carrying out espionage in collaboration with U.S. and Chiang Kai-shek spies." Liu Ren, Deng Tuo, Wu Han and Yue Songsheng died as a result of persecution.

(25) In January 1968, Zhang Chunqiao and Yao Wenyuan slandered the Shanghai Municipal Committee of the C.P.C., saying that it was a "stubborn bourgeois stronghold" and consisted of an "evil bunch." They falsely accused Chen Pixian, its first secretary, of being "an extremely cunning and treacherous counter-revolutionary double-dealer" and "the most dangerous enemy of the proletariat," and concocted the charge of "renegade" against Cao Diqiu, a secretary of the municipal Party committee and mayor of Shanghai. At the instigation and under the direction of Zhang Chunqiao and Yao Wenyuan, 17 people, who were secretaries or standing committee members of the Shanghai municipal committee of the Party and mayor or deputy mayors of the municipality, were falsely charged with being "renegades," "enemy agents," "capitalist roaders" or "counter-revolutionaries." Cao Diqiu and deputy mayor Jin Zhonghua died as a result of persecution.

(26) In December 1967, Chen Boda said in Tangshan that the C.P.C. organization in eastern Hebei Province "was probably a party embodying Kuomintang-Communist co-operation, and in fact it might be Kuomintang members and renegades who were playing a dominant role here." A case was trumped up at his instigation, and more than 84,000 Party cadres and masses in eastern Hebei Province were framed and persecuted. Zhang Wenhao and 2,955 others died as a result of persecution.

(27) On January 21, 1968, at the Jingxi Hotel in Beijing, Kang Sheng slandered Zhao Jianmin, secretary of the Yunnan Provincial Committee of the C.P.C., saying to his face, "You are a renegade ... I can tell. Forty years' experience in revolutionary work gives me this

kind of intuition . . . you have a deep-seated class hatred."
He falsely accused Zhao Jianmin of carrying out the plans
of a group of Kuomintang agents in Yunnan and of
"trying to take advantage of the Great Cultural Revolution to create chaos in the border areas." Kang Sheng
and Xie Fuzhi forbade Zhao Jianmin to argue, and Xie
announced there and then Zhao's arrest. Thus at the
instigation of Kang Sheng and Xie Fuzhi, the "case of
enemy agent Zhao Jianmin" was fabricated, leading to
the frame-up and persecution of large numbers of cadres
and masses in Yunnan, over 14,000 of whom died as a
result.

(28) Under the pretext of digging out the so-called
"Inner Mongolian People's Revolutionary Party," Kang
Sheng framed and persecuted large numbers of cadres
and masses in Inner Mongolia and sabotaged the unity
between the various nationalities. On February 4, 1968,
he said, "The Inner Mongolian People's Revolutionary
Party is still active underground. When we begin to fer-
ret out its members, we may overdo it a little, but we
needn't be worried about that." Again, on February 4,
1969, he said, "There are members of the Inner Mongolian People's Revolutionary Party inside the army too.
This is a very serious matter." Xie Fuzhi said, "The Inner Mongolian People's Revolutionary Party is disguised
as a Communist Party but actually it is not. We must
wipe it out." At the instigation of Kang Sheng and Xie
Fuzhi, more than 346,000 cadres and other people in the
Inner Mongolian Autonomous Region were framed and
persecuted in the case of the "Inner Mongolian People's
Revolutionary Party" and other false cases, and 16,222
persons died as a result of persecution.

(29) In 1967, Kang Sheng and others trumped up the
case of a "Xinjiang renegade clique." One hundred and
thirty-one Party cadres, who had been arrested and imprisoned in September 1942 by Sheng Shicai, the Xin-

jiang warlord, were falsely accused of having "surrendered to the enemy, betrayed the revolution" and "concealed themselves inside our Party" and of forming a "renegade clique." Ninety-two cadres, including Ma Mingfang, Zhang Ziyi, Yang Zhihua and Fang Zhichun, were persecuted, and Ma Mingfang and 25 others died as a result of persecution.

(30) In February 1946, in accordance with a decision of the Northeast Bureau of the C.P.C. Central Committee which had been approved by the Central Committee in 1945, Lu Zhengcao, Wan Yi, Zhang Xuesi, Jia Tao, Liu Lanbo, Li Youwen, Yu Yifu and 35 others jointly sent a telegraph to Chiang Kai-shek through the Xinhua News Agency in Yanan, demanding the release of Zhang Xueliang. From 1967 to 1969, the Lin Biao and Jiang Qing counter-revolutionary cliques and their key members distorted the facts about this incident, accused them of engaging in a "major, long premeditated, counter-revolutionary scheme to betray the Party and capitulate to the enemy" and fabricated the case of a "counter-revolutionary 'northeast gang' that betrayed the Party and capitulated to the enemy," framing and persecuting 90 persons. Zhang Xuesi, Jia Tao, Che Xiangchen and Chen Xianzhou died as a result of persecution.

(31) The counter-revolutionary cliques of Lin Biao and Jiang Qing falsely accused the underground organizations of the C.P.C. in Beiping, Shanghai, Tianjin, Guangdong, Sichuan, Yunnan and other places of having "recruited renegades" during the War of Resistance Against Japan and the Liberation War and of being a "Kuomintang," a "renegade party" and a "U.S.-Chiang special detachment." The Lin Biao and Jiang Qing counter-revolutionary cliques decided to "make the underground Party organizations the first target of attack." Consequently, large numbers of leaders and members of these underground Party organizations and

many ordinary people who had fought heroically against the enemy were charged with being "renegades," "hidden traitors," "Japanese agents," "Kuomintang agents," "U.S. agents," "spies" or "counter-revolutionaries."

In October 1967, Huang Yongsheng, in collusion with Liu Xingyuan, then political commissar of the Guangzhou Units of the P.L.A., and others, decided to investigate the history of the underground Party organization in Guangdong and set up a special group for this purpose. They slandered the underground Party organization as having "recruited renegades," and alleged that a number of "renegades," "enemy agents" and "spies" had sneaked in. This was the false case of "the Guangdong underground Party organization," which led to the framing and persecution of more than 7,100 people. Lin Qiangyun and 84 others died as a result of persecution.

(32) The Lin Biao counter-revolutionary clique trumped up false charges against large numbers of people in the P.L.A. Over 80,000 people were framed and persecuted, of whom 1,169 died.

From May 1967 to November 1970, Huang Yongsheng, in collusion with Liu Xingyuan, concocted the case of a "counter-revolutionary clique" in the Guangzhou Units of the P.L.A., falsely accusing Deputy Commander Wen Niansheng and others of attempting to "usurp power by staging a coup." More than 700 cadres were implicated. Wen Niansheng and some others died as a result of persecution.

Wu Faxian, in collusion with Wang Fei, then deputy chief of staff of the Air Force Command, and Liang Pu, its chief of staff, framed and persecuted large numbers of cadres and of the rank and file in the Air Force. Wu Faxian said, "If you don't strike them down, they will turn around and pounce on us and have us beheaded." He laid false charges against a number of leading cadres in the Air Force, alleging that they were "conducting underground activities" in an attempt to "seize power" and "stage a coup." Wu Faxian directly framed and persecuted 174 persons, among whom Gu Qian and Liu Shanben died as a result of persecution.

Li Zuopeng, in collusion with Wang Hongkun and Zhang Xiuchuan, framed and persecuted a large number of cadres and rank and file in the Navy. In January 1968, Li Zuopeng said that working on special cases was equivalent to "the Communist Party dealing blows at the Kuomintang." In October of the same year he again said that there should be "fierce attacks, vigorous charges and hot pursuit." Li Zuopeng directly framed and persecuted 120 persons, among whom Lei Yongtong and two others died as a result of persecution.

Qiu Huizuo, in league with Chen Pang, then deputy director of the General Logistics Department of the P.L.A., set up a kangaroo court in the department to extort confessions through torture. Qiu Huizuo said that there should be "ruthless struggle," "ruthless interrogation" and "ruthless dictatorship." Many of the cadres and of the rank and file were framed and persecuted. Qiu Huizuo directly framed and persecuted 462 people. Eight people, including Shen Maoxing and Wang Shuchen, died as a result of persecution.

(33) In order to suppress the "Workers' Red Detachment," a mass organization in Shanghai, and seize Party and government leadership there, Zhang Chunqiao made a phone call from Beijing to his wife, Li Wenjing, in Shanghai on December 28, 1966. He said, "The fruits of victory mustn't be snatched by the Red Detachment. Tell the revolutionary rebels that they mustn't just stand idly by." Li Wenjing informed Xu Jingxian, who then passed on the message. At the instigation of Zhang Chunqiao and others, Wang Hongwen worked in collusion with Geng Jinzhang, a criminal guilty of beating, smashing and looting, and organized and directed a number of peo-

ple who were ignorant of the real situation to attack the "Workers' Red Detachment." This armed clash, known as the Kangping Road Incident, resulted in 91 being injured or maimed.

On August 4, 1967, Wang Hongwen engineered and directed an armed attack on the mass organization known as the "Rebel Headquarters of the Revolutionary Alliance of the Shanghai Diesel Engine Plant." Six hundred and fifty people were imprisoned or injured. Afterwards, Zhang Chunqiao acclaimed Wang Hongwen as "our commanding officer" and "leader of the working class in Shanghai."

(34) In May 1967, while in Jinan, Zhang Chunqiao and Yao Wenyuan supported the suppression of the local masses by Wang Xiaoyu, then chairman of the Shandong Provincial Revolutionary Committee. Zhang told him, "You'll have my support if you're strong." Thereupon, on May 7, Wang Xiaoyu engineered a violent incident in the compound of the provincial revolutionary committee, resulting in the arrest and imprisonment of 388 persons. Later, Zhang Chunqiao and Yao Wenyuan again expressed their support for Wang Xiaoyu and congratulated him on his "victory in battle."

(35) In October 1966, Jiang Qing collaborated with Ye Qun in ordering Jiang Tengjiao to search and ransack the homes of a number of writers and artists in Shanghai. Ye Qun asked Wu Faxian to summon Jiang Tengjiao to Beijing, where she said to him, "One of Comrade Jiang Qing's letters has fallen into the hands of Zheng Junli, Gu Eryi and company. It's not clear who has the letter now, but you can organize some people to search the homes of five persons including Zheng Junli, Gu Eryi, Zhao Dan and Tong Zhiling. Bring me all the letters, diaries, notebooks and such like you can lay your hands on." And she added, "Keep this absolutely secret." After returning to Shanghai, Jiang Tengjiao got together more

than 40 people. They disguised themselves as Red Guards and, in the small hours of October 9, searched the homes of Zhao Dan, Zheng Junli, Tong Zhiling, Chen Liting and Gu Eryi. Jiang Tengjiao sent what they had seized in two batches to Ye Qun's residence in Beijing. In January 1967, under Jiang Qing's personal supervision, Xie Fuzhi and Ye Qun burnt all the letters, photos and other material relating to Jiang Qing, which had been obtained in the search.

(36) While in Shanghai in 1967, Zhang Chunqiao ordered a counter-revolutionary secret service organization — the "You Xuetao Group" (code named "244") — to undertake the special tasks of fascist espionage such as tailing, shadowing, kidnapping, ransacking people's homes, taking people into custody, secretly interrogating and torturing them, and gathering intelligence. From November 1967 to March 1968, this organization collected or fabricated for Zhang Chunqiao's use slanderous information on 97 leading cadres of the East China Bureau of the Central Committee of the C.P.C. It drew up a "Diagram Showing the Relationships Between Persons Working for the Sinister Line in the East China Bureau" and compiled 300 issues of the publications *Minesweeping Bulletin* and *Trends*. All told, it provided over one million words in intelligence material, trumping up cases to persecute 183 cadres and other people. In the winter of 1967 and the spring of 1968, this organization sent people to Jiangsu, Zhejiang and other places to carry out espionage. It falsely charged the leading Party, government and army cadres in eastern China with "organizing an underground armed detachment south of the Changjiang River" and "plotting a mutiny." On October 26, 1967, Wang Shaoyong, then vice-chairman of the Shanghai Municipal Revolutionary Committee, relayed Zhang Chunqiao's words to You Xuetao, "Be careful. You can spy on others, but they can spy on you too." In its "Sum-

mary of the Year's Work" submitted to Zhang Chunqiao on November 30, 1968, this organization said that it had been "fighting on a special front" and that "over the past year our work has been mainly covert struggle against the enemy. . . . From the central down to the local levels, we have directly or indirectly kicked the backsides of many bigshots." Zhang Chunqiao expressed his approval by writing "Thanks, Comrades" on the summary.

(37)   From 1974 to 1976, Jiang Qing, Zhang Chunqiao and Yao Wenyuan instructed Chi Qun and Xie Jingyi to use their base of activity at Qinghua University to make secret contacts and exchange information with key members of the Jiang Qing counter-revolutionary clique in certain departments of the Central Committee of the C.P.C. and the State Council and in Shanghai and Liaoning. They collected records of speeches made by leading cadres of provincial Party committees and documents of these committees and wrote up such material as *The Capitalist Roaders Are Still Travelling the Capitalist Road* and *Information for Reference* to frame leading Party, government and army cadres.

(38)   As a result of instigation and instructions from the Lin Biao and Jiang Qing counter-revolutionary cliques and their backbone elements, frame-ups were ubiquitous in the country. Numerous cadres and other people in the democratic parties, in people's organizations such as trade unions, the Communist Youth League and women's federations, and in cultural, educational, scientific, technological, journalistic, publishing, public health and physical culture circles were falsely charged and persecuted and disabled or died as a result, as did large numbers of returned overseas Chinese.

The following are the leading members of the democratic parties who were falsely charged and persecuted: Deng Baoshan, Vice-Chairman of the Central Committee of the Revolutionary Committee of the Kuomintang; Gao

Chongmin and Wu Han, Vice-Chairmen of the Central Committee of the China Democratic League; Sun Qimeng, Vice-Chairman of the Central Committee of the China Democratic National Construction Association; Che Xiangchen, Vice-Chairman of the Central Committee of the China Association for Promoting Democracy; Zhou Gucheng, member of the Presidium of the Central Committee of the Chinese Peasants' and Workers' Democratic Party; and Pan Shu, Vice-Chairman of the Central Committee of the Jiu San (September the Third) Society. Large numbers of standing committee members and members and alternate members of the central committees of the democratic parties as well as of the All-China Federation of Industry and Commerce were falsely charged and persecuted, among whom Huang Shaohong, Mei Gongbin, Chu Xichun, Gao Chongmin, Liu Qingyang, Pan Guangdan, Liu-Wang Liming, Liu Nianyi, Wang Xingyao, Tang Xunze, Xu Chongqing, Li Pingxin, Chen Linrui, Zheng Tianbao, Wang Jiaji, Liu Xiying, Zhang Xi, Wang Tianqiang and others died in consequence.

In the literary and art circles, more than 2,600 people were falsely charged and persecuted in the Ministry of Culture and units directly under it alone. Noted writers and well-known art workers including Lao She, Zhao Shuli, Zhou Xinfang, Gai Jiaotian, Pan Tianshou, Ying Yunwei, Zheng Junli and Sun Weishi died in consequence.

In the educational circles, more than 142,000 cadres and teachers in units under the Ministry of Education and in 17 provinces and municipalities were falsely charged and persecuted. Noted professors including Xiong Qinglai, Jian Bozan, He Sijing, Wang Shourong, Gu Yuzhen, Li Guangtian, Rao Yutai, Liu Pansui and Ma Te died in consequence of such persecution.

In scientific and technological circles, more than 53,000 scientists and technicians in units directly affiliated to the Chinese Academy of Sciences, two research institutes under the Seventh Ministry of Machine-Building and 17 provinces and municipalities were falsely charged and persecuted. Noted scientists such as geophysicist Zhao Jiuzhang, metallurgist Ye Zhupei, theoretical physicist Zhang Zongsui, entomologist Liu Chongle, taxonomist Chen Huanyong, and metal ceramist Zhou Ren died in consequence of such persecution.

In health circles, more than 500 of the 674 professors and associate professors in the 14 medical colleges and institutes directly led by the Ministry of Public Health were falsely charged and persecuted. Such famous medical scientists as pathologist Hu Zhengxiang, pharmacologist Zhang Changshao, specialist in thoracic surgery Ji Suhua, specialist in acupuncture Lu Shouyan, and traditional Chinese doctors Ye Xichun and Li Zhongren died as a result of persecution.

In physical culture circles, large numbers of cadres, coaches and sportsmen were falsely charged and persecuted. Outstanding coaches such as Fu Qifang, Rong Guotuan and Jiang Yongning were victimized and died.

Also falsely charged and persecuted were large numbers of national celebrated model workers, among whom Meng Tai and Shi Chuanxiang died in consequence.

In 19 provinces and municipalities, over 13,000 returned overseas Chinese and overseas Chinese family members were falsely charged and persecuted, of whom 281 died as a result. Such well-known figures in the field of overseas Chinese affairs as Fang Fang, Xu Li, Huang Jie, Chen Xujing, Huang Qinshu and Chen Manyun died as a result of their persecution.

Also persecuted on the false charges of being "renegades," "enemy agents," "counter-revolutionaries" or "lackeys of capitalist roaders" were innumerable cadres and other people working in Party, government and army organs, in enterprises and establishments, rural people's communes and production brigades and teams as well as in urban neighbourhood committees throughout the country.

III

Plotting to Assassinate Chairman Mao Zedong and Engineer an Armed Counter-Revolutionary Coup d'Etat

After the failure of their conspiracy to usurp Party and state leadership through "peaceful transition," the Lin Biao counter-revolutionary clique plotted to stage an armed counter-revolutionary coup d'etat and assassinate Chairman Mao Zedong.

(39) In October 1969, Lin Biao instructed Wu Faxian to make his son Lin Liguo deputy director of the General Office and concurrently deputy chief of the Operations Department of the Air Force Command. On October 18, Wu Faxian called together Lin Liguo, Wang Fei and Zhou Yuchi, another deputy director of the General Office of the Air Force Command, and said, "You are to report everything concerning the Air Force to Comrade Liguo. Everything is at his disposal and under his command." In this way Wu illegally put the Air Force under Lin Liguo's command. Zhou Yuchi and Wang Fei successively passed on this message to the standing committee of the Air Force Party committee at one of its working sessions and to the offices under the Air Force Command. Lin Liguo formed an "investigation group" in collaboration with Zhou Yuchi, Wang Fei and others. On the evening of May 2, 1970, when Lin Biao received Lin Liguo, Zhou Yuchi, Wang Fei and Liu Peifeng, then

a section head under the Air Force Command's General Office, he asked them who their leader was. On May 3, Zhou Yuchi, Wang Fei and others held a meeting to pledge allegiance to Lin Biao and made Lin Liguo their "leader." In October 1970, the "investigation group" headed by Lin Liguo was reorganized into a "joint fleet." Ye Qun gave code names to Zhou Yuchi, Wang Fei and others. The "joint fleet" constituted the backbone of Lin Biao's plot to assassinate Chairman Mao Zedong and stage an armed counter-revolutionary coup d'etat.

From 1970 to September 13, 1971, under the direction of Lin Liguo and Zhou Yuchi, Hu Ping, deputy chief-of-staff of the Air Force Command, Wang Weiguo, political commissar of P.L.A. Unit 7341, Mi Jianong, political commissar of the Guangzhou Branch of the Civil Aviation Administration of China (CAAC), Gu Tongzhou, chief-of-staff of the Guangzhou Air Force Headquarters and others set up secret centres of activity in Beijing, Shanghai and Guangzhou. These centres were used by Lin Liguo and others for liaison purposes and for storing arms and ammunition, wireless sets, bugging devices and confidential Party and government documents.

(40) From September 1970 onwards, Lin Biao stepped up his preparations for an armed counter-revolutionary coup d'etat. In February 1971, after plotting with Ye Qun and Lin Liguo in Suzhou, Lin Biao sent Lin Liguo to Shanghai, where from March 21 to 24, he called together such chief members of the "joint fleet" as Zhou Yuchi, Yu Xinye, a deputy section head under the General Office of the Air Force Command, and Li Weixin, then a deputy section head under the Political Department of P.L.A. Unit 7341, and mapped out a plan for an armed counter-revolutionary coup — *Outline of "Project 571."* They assessed the situation, worked out the outline of implementation and decided on the slogans and tactics. They

called for "gaining the upper hand by striking first militarily" and plotted to launch an armed counter-revolutionary coup d'etat to "seize nationwide political power" or bring about "a situation of rival regimes" by taking advantage of "some high-level meeting to catch all in one net" or "using special means such as bombs, the 543 (code name for a kind of guided missile — Tr.), traffic accidents, assassination, kidnapping and urban guerrilla squads." They also plotted to "seek Soviet help to tie down domestic and foreign forces."

On March 31, 1971, while in Shanghai, Lin Liguo, implementing the plan for establishing a "command team" as described in the *Outline of "Project 571*," summoned Jiang Tengjiao, Wang Weiguo, Chen Liyun, political commissar of the P.L.A. Unit 7350, and Zhou Jianping, deputy commander of the Nanjing Air Force, to a secret meeting at which Zhou Jianping was made "head" in Nanjing, Wang Weiguo "head" in Shanghai and Chen Liyun "head" in Hangzhou. Jiang Tengjiao was to be "responsible for liaison between the three places with a view to co-ordination and concerted operation."

In March 1971, instructed by Lin Liguo, Mi Jianong organized a "combat detachment" in Guangzhou. He made its members take an oath of allegiance to Lin Biao and Lin Liguo, and worked out argots and code words to be used in communications.

In April 1971, Lin Liguo directed Wang Weiguo to set up a "training corps" in Shanghai in preparation for the coup. Trainees were taught special skills in arresting people, hand-to-hand fighting, the use of various kinds of light weapons and driving motor vehicles.

(41) On the evening of September 5, 1971, Zhou Yuchi and Yu Xinye telephoned Gu Tongzhou to find out what Chairman Mao Zedong had said in Changsha to leading personnel. The information thus obtained was secretly

reported to Lin Liguo and Ye Qun at once, and Gu Tongzhou sent a written report to Ye Qun. On September 6, Li Zuopeng, then in Wuhan, received a confidential report from Liu Feng, political commissar of the P.L.A. Wuhan Units, containing Chairman Mao Zedong's conversations with leading personnel assembled in the city. Li Zuopeng returned to Beijing the same day and separately tipped off Huang Yongsheng and Qiu Huizuo. That very night Huang Yongsheng phoned Ye Qun about this, who was then in Beidaihe. After receiving the secret information from Gu Tongzhou and Huang Yongsheng, Lin Biao and Ye Qun made up their minds to assassinate Chairman Mao Zedong. On September 7, Lin Liguo issued the order for first-degree combat readiness to the "joint fleet." On September 8, Lin Biao issued the following handwritten order for the armed coup: "Expect you to act according to the order transmitted by Comrades Liguo and Yuchi." On the same day, Lin Liguo brought from Ye Qun in Beidaihe a sealed document addressed to Huang Yongsheng personally. It was to be delivered by Wang Fei. On the morning of September 10, Wang Fei delivered the sealed document to Huang Yongsheng. On the same day Huang Yongsheng repeatedly contacted Ye Qun, making five phone calls to her. The two longest lasted 90 and 135 minutes respectively. Also on that day, Liu Peifeng brought a letter to Huang Yongsheng from Lin Biao in Beidaihe, in which Lin wrote: "Comrade Yongsheng, I miss you very much and hope that you will always be optimistic at all times. Take care of your health. If you have any problems, consult Comrade Wang Fei directly." The letter was given to Wang Fei by Lin Liguo and Zhou Yuchi, and Wang was instructed to deliver it to Huang Yongsheng when necessary. From September 8 to 11, at their secret centres at the Air Force Academy and the Xijiao Airport of Beijing, Lin Liguo and Zhou Yuchi separately relayed Lin Biao's handwritten order for an armed coup to Liu Peifeng, Jiang Tengjiao, Wang Fei, Li Weixin, Lu Min, chief of the Operations Department of the Air Force Command, Liu Shiying, deputy director of its General Office, Cheng Hongzhen, secretary of the office, Guan Guanglie, political commissar of the P.L.A. Unit 0190, and others. They worked out the details for assassinating Chairman Mao Zedong. Jiang Tengjiao was appointed frontline commander for action in the Shanghai area. They plotted to attack Chairman Mao Zedong's train with flame throwers and 40-mm. bazookas, dynamite the Shuofang Railway Bridge near Suzhou, bomb the train from the air, or blow up the oil depot in Shanghai, near which the special train would pull up, and then assassinate the Chairman in the ensuing commotion, or let Wang Weiguo carry out the murder when he was being received by Chairman Mao Zedong.

Meanwhile, Lin Biao and Ye Qun were making preparations for fleeing south to Guangzhou to set up a separate Party central committee, and also for defecting to another country. On September 10, they ordered Zhou Yuchi and others to obtain from the Air Force Command maps showing where radar units were deployed in north, northeast and northwest China, frequency tables of the radio stations in neighbouring countries which could be used for navigation purposes, maps showing air lines leading from Beijing to Ulan Bator and Irkutsk and the location of their airports and the latter's call signs and radio frequency tables, as well as information concerning the airports in the Guangzhou and Fuzhou areas.

(42) On the evening of September 11, Wang Weiguo secretly telephoned Lin Liguo and Zhou Yuchi, informing them that Chairman Mao Zedong had already left Shanghai for Beijing. When Lin Biao and Ye Qun learned that their plot to murder Chairman Mao Zedong had fallen through, they planned to flee south to Guangzhou, taking

along Huang Yongsheng, Wu Faxian, Li Zuopeng and Qiu Huizuo, and set up a separate Party central committee there to split the nation. They also planned to "launch a pincer attack from north and south in alliance with the Soviet Union should fighting be necessary." On September 12, Lin Liguo and Zhou Yuchi separately told Jiang Tengjiao, Wang Fei, Yu Xinye, Hu Ping and Wang Yongkui, a deputy section chief in the Intelligence Department of the Air Force Command, to make preparations for the flight south. Hu Ping and company had eight planes ready to leave for Guangzhou and helped Lin Liguo to fly to Shanhaiguan on special plane 256, which was then assigned for the use of Lin Biao, Ye Qun and Lin Liguo in Beidaihe. Wang Fei, Yu Xinye and He Dequan, chief of the Intelligence Department of the Air Force Command, prepared the name list of those who were to flee south, assigned duties and made specific plans for action. Around 10 o'clock that evening, Premier Zhou Enlai inquired about the details concerning the flight of special plane 256 to Shanhaiguan and ordered it to return to Beijing at once. Hu Ping lied, saying that the plane was on a training flight to Shanhaiguan and had developed engine trouble. Thus he refused to carry out Premier Zhou's order. Meanwhile, he telephoned Zhou Yuchi and tipped him off on what had happened.

Late at night on September 12, Lin Biao, Ye Qun and Lin Liguo received a secret report that Premier Zhou Enlai had been making inquiries about the special plane. Thereupon, they hurried to the Shanhaiguan Airport with Liu Peifeng and others, scrambled on to the plane and ordered it to start taxiing without waiting for the co-pilot, navigator and radio operator to board and the lights to be turned on. The aircraft took off at 00:32 hours on September 13 and crashed near Undur Khan in Mongolia, killing all those aboard.

At 03:15 hours on September 13, 1971, Zhou Yuchi, Yu Xinye and Li Weixing hijacked helicopter 3685 at the Shahe Airport in Beijing in an attempt to flee the country, taking with them piles of confidential state documents and large amounts of U.S. dollars which they had illicitly obtained. After seeing through their intention, pilot Chen Xiuwen took steps to fly the helicopter back to Huairou County, a suburb of Beijing, but was killed by Zhou Yuchi when the helicopter landed.

(43) Before Lin Biao's defection, Premier Zhou Enlai had made the decision that special plane 256 "cannot take off without a joint order from four persons," namely, Zhou Enlai, Huang Yongsheng, Wu Faxian and Li Zuopeng. However, Li Zuopeng distorted this directive when relaying it to those in charge of the Navy's Shanhaiguan Airport, saying, "The plane must not be allowed to take off unless one of the four leading officials gives the order." He added, "If anyone gives you such an order, you must report it to me. You will be held responsible." At 00:20 hours on September 13, when special plane 256 was getting ready to take off but its engines were not yet started, the airport leadership phoned Li Zuopeng asking what they should do if the plane were to insist on taking off. Instead of taking any measures to prevent the plane from taking off, Li Zuopeng said evasively, "You may report directly to the Premier and ask for his instructions." He was procrastinating so that Lin Biao could have enough time to escape. Afterwards, Li Zuopeng tried to cover up his crime by altering the logbook entry of the relevant phone calls.

(44) After Lin Biao's defection on September 13, 1971, Huang Yongsheng, Wu Faxian, Qiu Huizuo and others separately destroyed incriminating evidence, including their correspondence with Lin Biao and Ye Qun, notebooks, photographs and other material, in an attempt to cover up the crimes of the counter-revolutionary clique.

IV

Plotting Armed Rebellion in Shanghai

Zhang Chunqiao, Yao Wenyuan and Wang Hongwen, as well as Ma Tianshui, Xu Jingxian, Wang Xiuzhen and company, made Shanghai their base, built up their own armed force and plotted an armed rebellion in the face of their impending doom.

(45) In July 1967, Zhang Chunqiao wrote in a report he finalized, "We must use the gun to protect revolution made with the pen" and instructed Wang Hongwen and others to organize an armed force in Shanghai under their control. In September 1973, Wang Hongwen said to Wang Xiuzhen, "A national general headquarters must be set up for the people's militia. I will take charge of it myself." In March 1974, Wang again told her, "The army must not be allowed to lead the militia whose command should be in the hands of the [Shanghai] municipal Party committee." On many occasions in January and August 1975, Wang Hongwen told Ma Tianshui, Xu Jingxian and Wang Xiuzhen in Beijing and Shanghai, "What worries me most is that the army is not in our hands." He added, "We must be on the alert against the danger of the revisionists taking power" and "We must be prepared for guerrilla warfare." In February 1976, he said, "It's Chunqiao and I who organized the People's Militia in Shanghai." And he added, "I'm certainly going to keep firm control over it. You must run it well for me. . . . The army isn't so reliable."

(46) On May 7, 1976, when talking in Beijing with Chen Jide, a member of the Shanghai Writing Group, Yao Wenyuan said, "The Great Cultural Revolution is an example of violence, so is the Tian An Men Square Incident. And the outcome of future struggles will have to be decided through violence too." On returning to Shanghai, Chen Jide communicated Yao's views to Ma Tianshui, Xu

Jingxian and others. In August of the same year, Yao Wenyuan personally revised and approved an article by the Shanghai Writing Group, entitled "Strengthen the Building of the Workers' Militia," which was later published in *Hongqi* (*Red Flag*). To prepare public opinion for violent suppression and armed rebellion, the article called for the struggle of the workers' militia against "the bourgeoisie inside the Party."

(47) In August 1976, Ding Sheng, head of the Nanjing Units of the P.L.A., arrived in Shanghai and had a secret talk with Ma Tianshui, Xu Jingxian and Wang Xiuzhen at Yanan Hotel till midnight. Ding Sheng said, "My biggest worry is Unit 6453. . . . I haven't the slightest control over it. . . . Several of its divisions are deployed along the Wuxi-Suzhou-Shanghai line. This is a big headache. . . . You must be prepared for any eventuality." Immediately afterwards, Ma Tianshui attended to the arming of the militia. Altogether, 74,220 rifles, 300 artillery pieces and more than 10 million rounds of ammunition were handed out in no time, as a concrete measure in preparation for an armed rebellion. On September 21 of the same year, Zhang Chunqiao received Xu Jingxian alone in Beijing. After hearing about Ding Sheng's secret talk with Ma Tianshui, Xu Jingxian and Wang Xiuzhen in Shanghai and about the hurried handout of weapons, Zhang Chunqiao said, "Be careful, keep your eyes open for new trends in the class struggle." On September 23, Wang Hongwen made a telephone call to Wang Xiuzhen, saying, "Be on your guard, for the struggle isn't over yet. The bourgeoisie inside the Party will not be reconciled to defeat. Someone or other is sure to try to reinstate Deng Xiaoping."

(48) On October 6, 1976, the gang of Jiang Qing, Zhang Chunqiao, Yao Wenyuan and Wang Hongwen was smashed. On October 8, Xu Jingxian and Wang Xiuzhen sent to Beijing Miao Wenjin, secretary of Jin Zumin, who was

in charge of the preparatory group for the reorganization of the All-China Federation of Trade Unions, to find out what had happened. They adopted a secret code for contact purposes. That evening, Miao Wenjin and Zhu Jiayao, a member of the leading Party group in the Ministry of Public Security, made a phone call to Kang Ningyi, political commissar of the Security Section of the Shanghai Municipal Committee of the C.P.C., asking him to tell Wang Xiuzhen that the worst had befallen Jiang Qing, Zhang Chunqiao, Yao Wenyuan and Wang Hongwen, using the formula "My mother has contracted myocardial infarction." Soon afterwards, Zhu Jiayao phoned Kang Ningyi again, asking him to tell Wang Xiuzhen, "People have been assembled and locked up. They can no longer move about." So Xu Jingxian and Wang Xiuzhen immediately called an emergency mobilization meeting. They decided to "fight it out." They said, "Send the militia into action. If we cannot keep up the fight for a week, five or three days will suffice to let the whole world know what's happening." There and then, Xu Jingxian wrote an order to assemble and deploy 33,500 militiamen. A command team and two secret command posts were set up for the armed rebellion, and the newspapers and broadcasting stations in Shanghai were instructed to act in co-ordination. Li Binshan, deputy political commissar of the Shanghai Garrison, Shi Shangying and Zhong Dingdong, who were in charge of the Shanghai militia headquarters, and others drew up an initial plan for the armed rebellion, which was then approved by Wang Xiuzhen. Xue Ganqing and Xu Chenghu, deputy secretaries of the Party committee of the Shanghai Municipal Public Security Bureau, worked out the bureau's programme for action. On October 9, Shi Shangying called a meeting of the militia leaders of ten districts and of the five militia divisions directly under the command of the Shanghai Municipal Revolutionary Committee and ordered them to muster their forces and see to it that there were enough motor vehicles and drivers and that their arms and ammunition matched. Over 27,000 rifles and artillery pieces and 225 motor vehicles were assigned for use. A large quantity of food and other material was made available. Fifteen transmitter-receivers were installed at the command posts in the Jiangnan Shipyards and the China Textile Machinery Plant and at the militia headquarters of the various districts so as to link them up through telecommunications. Zhong Dingdong drew up more specific operation plans, code named "Han No. 1" and "Fang No. 2," for the armed rebellion. They decided to throw up three cordons between the heart of Shanghai and its outskirts in order to bring under control the city's administrative centre, railway stations, wharves, airports, harbours, the Pujiang River Tunnel, bridges and other main transport routes. Pass words and argots were also worked out. On October 12, they planned to publish a "Message to the People of Shanghai and the Whole Country" and drafted 21 counter-revolutionary slogans. On the evening of the same day, Wang Shaoyong and Zhu Yongjia, together with Huang Tao and Chen Ada, who were leading members of the group in charge of industry and communications under the Shanghai Municipal Revolutionary Committee, and others met to plan production stoppages through strikes, parades and demonstrations, the acquiring of control over the press and radio stations and blockade of the news released by the central media. They planned to cut off the supply of electricity at the grid, barricade airport runways with steel ingots and scuttle ships to block the river mouth at Wusongkou. They put forward the counter-revolutionary slogans: "Return Jiang Qing to us," "Return Chunqiao to us,"

"Return Wenyuan to us" and "Return Hongwen to us," readying themselves for "a life-and-death struggle."

The above-mentioned facts establish that the two counter-revolutionary cliques of Lin Biao and Jiang Qing framed and persecuted the Chairman of the People's Republic of China, the Chairman of the Standing Committee of the National People's Congress, the Premier of the State Council, the General Secretary of the Central Committee of the Chinese Communist Party and other leaders of the Party and state, persecuted and suppressed large numbers of cadres and people, plotted to assassinate Chairman Mao Zedong and planned to engineer an armed rebellion, and that they are counter-revolutionary cliques whose aim was to overthrow the political power of the dictatorship of the proletariat. Their felonies have been proved by a mass of conclusive evidence. The people of all nationalities, and in particular, the large numbers of cadres and other people who were framed, persecuted or implicated, are witnesses to their criminal activities. And so are those who, for a time, were hoodwinked or misled by them.

In accordance with the provisions of Article 9 of the Criminal Law of the People's Republic of China with regard to the standard for the application of law, this procuratorate affirms that the following ten principal culprits have violated the Criminal Law of the People's Republic of China and have committed the crime of attempting to overthrow the government and split the state, the crime of attempting to engineer an armed rebellion, the crime of having people injured or murdered for counter-revolutionary ends, the crime of framing and persecuting people for counter-revolutionary ends, the crime of organizing and leading counter-revolutionary cliques, the crime of conducting demagogical propaganda for counter-revolutionary ends, the crime of extorting confessions by torture, and the crime of illegally detaining people, and that they should be duly prosecuted according to their criminal liability. This Procuratorate hereby institutes, according to law, a public prosecution against the following ten principal accused:

Defendant Jiang Qing, female, 67, of Zhucheng County, Shandong Province. Member of the Tenth Central Committee of the Communist Party of China and its Political Bureau prior to her arrest. Now in custody;

Defendant Zhang Chunqiao, male, 63, of Juye County, Shandong Province. Member of the Tenth Central Committee of the C.P.C., its Political Bureau and the Bureau's Standing Committee, vice-premier of the State Council, director of the General Political Department of the Chinese People's Liberation Army, first secretary of the Shanghai Municipal Committee of the C.P.C., and chairman of the Shanghai Municipal Revolutionary Committee prior to his arrest. Now in custody;

Defendant Yao Wenyuan, male, 49, of Zhuji County, Zhejiang Province. Member of the Tenth Central Committee of the C.P.C. and its Political Bureau, second secretary of the Shanghai Municipal Committee of the C.P.C., and vice-chairman of the Shanghai Municipal Revolutionary Committee prior to his arrest. Now in custody;

Defendant Wang Hongwen, male, 45, of Changchun, Jilin Province. Member of the Tenth Central Committee of the C.P.C., its Political Bureau and the Bureau's Standing Committee, vice-chairman of the Central Committee of the C.P.C., secretary of the Shanghai Municipal Committee of the C.P.C., and vice-chairman of the Shanghai Municipal Revolutionary Committee prior to his arrest. Now in custody;

Defendant Chen Boda, male, 76, of Huian County, Fujian Province. Member of the Ninth Central Committee of the C.P.C., its Political Bureau and the Bureau's Standing Committee prior to his arrest. Now in custody;

Defendant Huang Yongsheng, male, 70, of Xianning County, Hubei Province. Member of the Ninth Central Committee of the C.P.C. and its Political Bureau, and chief of the General Staff of the P.L.A. prior to his arrest. Now in custody;

Defendant Wu Faxian, male, 65, of Yongfeng County, Jiangxi Province. Member of the Ninth Central Committee of the C.P.C. and its Political Bureau, and deputy chief of the P.L.A. General Staff and concurrently commander of the P.L.A. Air Force prior to his arrest. Now in custody;

Defendant Li Zuopeng, male, 66, of Jian County, Jiangxi Province. Member of the Ninth Central Committee of the C.P.C. and its Political Bureau, and deputy chief of the P.L.A. General Staff and concurrently first political commissar of the P.L.A. Navy prior to his arrest. Now in custody;

Defendant Qiu Huizuo, male, 66, of Xingguo County, Jiangxi Province. Member of the Ninth Central Committee of the C.P.C. and its Political Bureau, and deputy chief of the P.L.A. General Staff and concurrently director of the P.L.A. General Logistics Department prior to his arrest. Now in custody; and

Defendant Jiang Tengjiao, male, 61, of Hongan County, Hubei Province. Air Force political commissar of the P.L.A. Nanjing Units prior to his arrest. Now in custody.

In accordance with Item 5, Article 11, of the Law of Criminal Procedure of the People's Republic of China, no criminal liability shall be pursued against those defendants who are dead. In this case, they are Lin Biao, Kang Sheng, Xie Fuzhi, Ye Qun, Lin Liguo and Zhou Yuchi, who were also principal culprits of the Lin Biao and Jiang Qing counter-revolutionary cliques. The other defendants involved in this will be dealt with separately.

Huang Huoqing

Chief Procurator of the Supreme People's Procuratorate of the People's Republic of China and concurrently Chief of the Special Procuratorate Under the Supreme People's Procuratorate

November 2, 1980

WRITTEN JUDGEMENT
OF
THE SPECIAL COURT UNDER
THE SUPREME PEOPLE'S COURT OF
THE PEOPLE'S REPUBLIC OF CHINA

Te Fa Zi No. 1

The prosecutors: Huang Huoqing, Chief Procurator of the Supreme People's Procuratorate and concurrently Chief of the Special Procuratorate; Yu Ping and Shi Jinqian, Deputy Chiefs of the Special Procuratorate; and Procurators Ma Chunyi, Wang Wenlin, Wang Fang, Wang Zhenzhong, Wang Pusheng, Wang Yaoqing, Feng Changyi, Qu Wenda, Zhu Zongzheng, Jiang Wen, Sun Shufeng, Li Tianxiang, Shen Jialiang, Zhang Zhongru, Zhang Yingjie, Zhang Zhaoqi, Meng Qingen, Tu Men, Zhong Shuqin, Yuan Tongjiang and Jing Yusong.

The defendant, Jiang Qing, female, 67, of Zhucheng County, Shandong Province. Formerly deputy head of the "cultural revolution group under the Central Committee" of the Communist Party of China and a member of the Political Bureau of the Ninth and Tenth C.P.C. Central Committees. Now in custody.

The defendant, Zhang Chunqiao, male, 63, of Juye County, Shandong Province. Formerly deputy head of the "cultural revolution group under the C.P.C. Central Committee," a member of the Political Bureau of the

Ninth C.P.C. Central Committee, a Standing Committee member of the Political Bureau of the Tenth C.P.C. Central Committee and chairman of the Shanghai Municipal Revolutionary Committee. Now in custody.

The defendant, Yao Wenyuan, male, 49, of Zhuji County, Zhejiang Province. Formerly a member of the "cultural revolution group under the C.P.C. Central Committee," a member of the Political Bureau of the Ninth and Tenth C.P.C. Central Committees and vice-chairman of the Shanghai Municipal Revolutionary Committee. Now in custody.

The defendant, Wang Hongwen, male, 46, of Changchun city, Jilin Province. Formerly vice-chairman of the Tenth C.P.C. Central Committee and vice-chairman of the Shanghai Municipal Revolutionary Committee. Now in custody.

The defendant, Chen Boda, male, 76, of Huian County, Fujian Province. Formerly head of the "cultural revolution group under the C.P.C. Central Committee" and a Standing Committee member of the Political Bureau of the Eighth and Ninth C.P.C. Central Committees. Now in custody.

The defendant, Huang Yongsheng, male, 70, of Xianning County, Hubei Province. Formerly chief of the General Staff of the Chinese People's Liberation Army. Now in custody.

The defendant, Wu Faxian, male, 65, of Yongfeng County, Jiangxi Province. Formerly deputy chief of the P.L.A. General Staff and concurrently commander of the Air Force. Now in custody.

The defendant, Li Zuopeng, male, 66, of Ji'an County, Jiangxi Province. Formerly deputy chief of the P.L.A. General Staff and concurrently first political commissar of the Navy. Now in custody.

The defendant, Qiu Huizuo, male, 66, of Xingguo

County, Jiangxi Province. Formerly deputy chief of the P.L.A. General Staff and concurrently director of the General Logistics Department. Now in custody.

The defendant, Jiang Tengjiao, male, 61, of Hongan County, Hubei Province. Formerly air force political commissar of the P.L.A. Nanjing Units. Now in custody.

The advocates: Defence lawyers Han Xuezhang and Zhang Zhong for the defendant Yao Wenyuan;

Defence lawyers Gan Yupei and Fu Zhiren for the defendant Chen Boda;

Defence lawyers Ma Kechang and Zhou Hengyuan for the defendant Wu Faxian;

Defence lawyers Zhang Sizhi and Su Huiyu for the defendant Li Zuopeng;

Defence lawyers Wang Shunhua and Zhou Kuizheng for the defendant Jiang Tengjiao.

The other defendants, Jiang Qing, Zhang Chunqiao, Wang Hongwen, Huang Yongsheng and Qiu Huizuo, did not entrust their defence to any lawyers, nor did they request the Special Court to assign advocates for them.

Task of the Special Court

The Special Court Under the Supreme People's Court of the People's Republic of China was set up in line with the "decision on the establishment of a Special Procuratorate Under the Supreme People's Procuratorate and a Special Court Under the Supreme People's Court to prosecute and try the principal defendants in the case of the Lin Biao and Jiang Qing counter-revolutionary cliques," which was adopted at the 16th Meeting of the Standing Committee of the Fifth National People's Congress held on September 29, 1980. The task of this court, as defined by the decision, is trying the principal defendants in the case of the Lin Biao and Jiang Qing counter-revolutionary cliques.

On November 5, 1980, the Special Procuratorate brought before this court the case of the Lin Biao and Jiang Qing counter-revolutionary cliques plotting to overthrow the political power of the dictatorship of the proletariat, and lodged a public prosecution against the defendants, Jiang Qing, Zhang Chunqiao, Yao Wenyuan, Wang Hongwen, Chen Boda, Huang Yongsheng, Wu Faxian, Li Zuopeng, Qiu Huizuo and Jiang Tengjiao.

Article 9 of the Criminal Law of the People's Republic of China states: "If an act performed after the founding of the People's Republic of China and prior to the enforcement of the present law was not deemed an offence under the laws, decrees and policies then in force, these laws, decrees and policies shall be the standard. If the act was deemed an offence under the said laws, decrees and policies and is also subject to prosecution under Section 8, Chapter 4, of the general provisions of the present law, the standard of criminal liability shall also be the said laws, decrees and policies. But if the act is not deemed an offence or the penalty for the offence is lighter under the present law, the present law shall apply." In line with the Criminal Law of the People's Republic of China and the Law of Criminal Procedure of the People's Republic of China, this court tried the principal defendants in the case of the Lin Biao and Jiang Qing counter-revolutionary cliques in Beijing from November 20, 1980, to January 25, 1981. This court listened to the speeches of public prosecutors in support of the public prosecution, interrogated the defendants and listened to their depositions, defences and final statements, heard the speeches of the advocates, the testimonies of the witnesses and the accounts of some of the victims, and verified various pieces of evidence directly relating to the case.

This court confirms that the counter-revolutionary clique headed by Lin Biao and the counter-revolutionary clique headed by Jiang Qing were both counter-revolutionary cliques that carried out conspiratorial activities for the purpose of seizing the supreme power of the Party and the state. These two counter-revolutionary cliques had the common criminal motives and purpose of overthrowing the people's democratic dictatorship, namely the dictatorship of the proletariat (including the state organs and military institutions and, in the present case, also including the Chinese Communist Party, the force that exercises leadership over the above-mentioned organs and institutions) in China, conspired together in committing criminal offences, and thus formed a counter-revolutionary alliance. The principal culprits in the case of the Lin Biao and Jiang Qing counter-revolutionary cliques are the defendants, Jiang Qing, Zhang Chunqiao, Yao Wenyuan, Wang Hongwen, Chen Boda, Huang Yongsheng, Wu Faxian, Li Zuopeng, Qiu Huizuo and Jiang Tengjiao, as well as the following who are dead: Lin Biao (formerly vice-chairman of the Eighth and Ninth C.P.C. Central Committees and minister of national defence), Kang Sheng (formerly advisor to the "cultural revolution group under the C.P.C. Central Committee" and vice-chairman of the Tenth C.P.C. Central Committee), Xie Fuzhi (formerly a member of the Political Bureau of the Ninth C.P.C. Central Committee and minister of public security), Ye Qun (formerly a member of the Political Bureau of the Ninth C.P.C. Central Committee and the wife of Lin Biao), Lin Liguo (formerly deputy chief of the Operations Department of the P.L.A. Air Force Headquarters and the son of Lin Biao) and Zhou Yuchi (formerly deputy director of the General Office of the P.L.A. Air Force Headquarters).

It was in the decade of turmoil known as the "great cultural revolution" that the Lin Biao and Jiang Qing counter-revolutionary cliques carried out their counter-revolutionary criminal activities. During the "great cultural revolution," the political life of the state became extremely abnormal, and the socialist legal system was seriously undermined. Taking advantage of their positions and power at that time and resorting to every possible means, overt and covert, by pen and by gun, the Lin Biao and Jiang Qing counter-revolutionary cliques framed and persecuted state leaders and leaders of the Chinese Communist Party and the democratic parties in a premeditated way, conspired to overthrow the government and sabotage the army, suppressed and persecuted large numbers of cadres, intellectuals and ordinary people from various social strata, poisoned the minds of large numbers of young people, and endangered the life and property and right of autonomy of the people of various national minorities. The Lin Biao counter-revolutionary clique plotted to stage an armed coup d'etat and conspired to assassinate Chairman Mao Zedong. The Jiang Qing counter-revolutionary clique plotted to stage an armed rebellion in Shanghai. The criminal activities of the Lin Biao and Jiang Qing counter-revolutionary cliques lasted for a whole decade, bringing calamities to all fields of work and all regions across the country, subjecting the system of the people's democratic dictatorship and socialist public order in our country to extraordinarily grave danger, inflicting very great damage upon the national economy and all other undertakings, and causing enormous disasters to the people of all nationalities in the country.

The acts of the principal culprits in the case of the Lin Biao and Jiang Qing counter-revolutionary cliques, which endangered the state and society, constitute criminal offences both under the laws and decrees then in force and under the Criminal Law of the People's Republic of China which came into force on January 1, 1980. The duty of this court is to hear the criminal offences committed by the principal culprits in the case of the Lin Biao and Jiang Qing counter-revolutionary cliques and pursue their criminal liability, in strict accordance with the Criminal Law of the People's Republic of China. This court does not handle other problems of the defendants that do not fall into the category of criminal offences.

Criminal Offences by the Principal Culprits of the Lin-Jiang Cliques

The offences committed by the principal culprits in the case of the Lin Biao and Jiang Qing counter-revolutionary cliques are as follows:

The Lin Biao and Jiang Qing counter-revolutionary cliques plotted to subvert the government and overthrow the people's democratic dictatorship in China. While formulating the policy for seizing Party and state leadership, Lin Biao said on January 23, 1967: "All power, be it at the top, middle or lower levels, should be seized. In some cases, this should be done soon, in others later. . . . This may be done at the top or lower levels, or done in co-ordination at both levels." Zhang Chunqiao said on January 22: "We must seize power everywhere." From 1967 to 1975, Zhang Chunqiao declared on many occasions that "the 'great cultural revolution' " meant "a change of dynasty." Although the above-mentioned counter-revolutionary aim of the Lin Biao and Jiang Qing counter-revolutionary cliques could not entirely succeed owing to resistance from the Party, the government and the people, they did succeed over a fairly long period of time in seriously disrupting government institutions and affecting their work, seriously undermining the people's public security organs, the people's procuratorates and the people's courts. They controlled leadership in the departments of organization and propaganda under the Central Committee of the Communist Party of China, and the departments of culture, education, health, and nationalities affairs under the State Council, seized leadership in most of the provinces, autonomous regions and municipalities directly under the central government, and for a time "smashed" the General Political Department of the Chinese People's Liberation Army and seized part of the leadership in some military institutions.

The Lin Biao and Jiang Qing counter-revolutionary cliques worked hand in glove in scheming to frame and persecute Liu Shaoqi, Chairman of the People's Republic of China. In August of 1966, Lin Biao asked Ye Qun to dictate to Lei Yingfu, deputy director of the Operations Department of the Headquarters of the P.L.A. General Staff, material containing false charges they had fabricated against Liu Shaoqi, and they instructed Lei Yingfu to put these charges in writing. In December of the same year, Zhang Chunqiao privately summoned Kuai Dafu, a student at Qinghua University, and instigated him to organize a demonstration and agitate first of all in society at large for "overthrowing Liu Shaoqi." In July of 1967, Jiang Qing, in collusion with Kang Sheng and Chen Boda, decided to have Liu Shaoqi persecuted physically, depriving him of his freedom of action ever since. Beginning from May of 1967, Jiang Qing assumed direct control of the "group for inquiring into the special case of Liu Shaoqi and Wang Guangmei" and, in collusion with Kang Sheng and Xie Fuzhi, directed the group to extort confessions from people arrested and imprisoned and rig up false evidence vilifying Liu Shaoqi as a "renegade," "enemy agent" and "counter-revolutionary." In 1967, in order to fabricate false evidence against Liu Shaoqi, Jiang Qing made the decision to arrest and imprison Yang Yi-chen, Deputy Governor of Hebei Province (formerly a worker in the organization department of the C.P.C. Manchuria provincial committee), Yang Chengzuo, a professor at the China People's University (formerly a professor at the Catholic University in Beijing and Wang Guangmei's teacher); Wang Guangen, a citizen of Tianjin (formerly assistant manager of the Fengtian Cotton Mill); Hao Miao, Liu Shaoqi's cook, and seven others. When Yang Chengzuo was critically ill, Jiang Qing said to members of the special case group: "Step up the interrogation to squeeze out of him what we need before he dies." As a result of this decision made by Jiang Qing, Yang Chengzuo was hounded to death. The special case group under her control also persecuted Wang Guangen to death. In collusion with Xie Fuzhi, Jiang Qing ordered people to extort confessions repeatedly from Zhang Zhongyi, a professor at the Hebei Beijing Normal College (formerly a professor at the Catholic University in Beijing and Wang Guangmei's teacher), who was critically ill, so that he died barely two hours after an interrogation to extort confessions from him. In order to rig up false evidence and frame Liu Shaoqi as a "renegade," Jiang Qing, along with Kang Sheng, Xie Fuzhi and others, ordered the special case group to extort confessions from Ding Juequn, who worked with Liu Shaoqi in the workers' movement in Wuhan in 1927, and Meng Yongqian, who was arrested at the same time as Liu Shaoqi in Shenyang in 1929. As a result of the framing by Jiang Qing and others, Liu Shaoqi was imprisoned and persecuted to death.

The Lin Biao and Jiang Qing counter-revolutionary cliques framed and persecuted other Party and state leaders. In July of 1967, Qi Benyu, a member of the "cultural revolution group under the C.P.C. Central Committee," with the approval of Kang Sheng, instigated Han Aijing, a student at the Beijing Aeronautical Engineering Institute, to subject Peng Dehuai, a Member of the Political Bureau of the C.P.C. Central Committee, to physical persecution. As a result, Peng Dehuai was severely wounded with several ribs fractured. On November 3, 1970, Huang Yongsheng agreed to the proposal raised by the group in charge of the special case of Peng Dehuai, that Peng Dehuai be "sentenced to life imprisonment and deprived of civil rights for life," in order to continue persecuting him. Peng Dehuai was later tormented to death because of the framing and persecution by the Lin Biao and Jiang Qing counter-revolutionary cliques. In July of 1966, Kang Sheng falsely charged He Long, Vice-Premier and Vice-Chairman of the Military Commission of the C.P.C. Central Committee, with "deploying troops to stage a February mutiny" in Beijing. In August of the same year, Lin Biao instructed Wu Faxian to fabricate charges against He Long. In April of 1968, Li Zuopeng and others falsely charged He Long and others with "usurping army leadership and opposing the Party." Framed by Lin Biao, Kang Sheng and others, He Long was imprisoned and tormented to death. On June 23, 1967, Huang Yongsheng approved the "report for instruction on investigation for the purpose of rounding up renegades," which was submitted by the head of the military control commission stationed in the Guangzhou Municipal Public Security Bureau, and its appendix, "plan for investigation, No. 1," in a scheme to frame Ye Jianying, Vice-Chairman of the Military Commission of the C.P.C. Central Committee, as a "renegade." In June of 1968, Huang Yongsheng turned over to Ye Qun the materials charging Ye Jianying with "plotting a counter-revolutionary coup." In August of 1968, Huang Yongsheng and Wu Faxian fabricated facts and framed Luo Ruiqing, Vice-Premier of the State Council, as a "counter-revolutionary who has committed heinous crimes." From late 1966 to 1968, Chen Boda on quite a few occasions framed Lu Dingyi, Vice-Premier of the State Council, as an "active counter-revolutionary," "renegade" and "hidden traitor," and decided to have his health ruined.

On July 21, 1968, Jiang Qing and Kang Sheng drew up a list of names, aiming at framing Members of the Eighth C.P.C. Central Committee. In August of the same year, Kang Sheng again drew up lists of names aimed at framing Members of the Standing Committee of the Third National People's Congress and Standing Committee Members of the Fourth National Committee of the Chinese People's Political Consultative Conference. In December of the same year, Xie Fuzhi rigged up the case of a "Chinese communist party (Marxist-Leninist)" with still another list of names. On these four lists, 103 Members and Alternate Members of the Eighth C.P.C. Central Committee, 52 Members of the Third N.P.C. Standing Committee and 76 Standing Committee Members of the Fourth C.P.P.C.C. National Committee were labelled "enemy agents," "renegades," "elements having illicit relations with foreign countries," "counter-revolutionaries," "suspected renegades" or "suspected enemy agents." The people framed were subsequently persecuted. They included the Chairman and seven Vice-Chairmen of the N.P.C. Standing Committee, 12 Vice-Premiers of the State Council, 22 Members and Alternate Members of the Political Bureau of the C.P.C. Central Committee, the General Secretary and 13 Members and Alternate Members of the Secretariat of the C.P.C. Central Committee, six Vice-Chairmen of the Military Commission of the C.P.C. Central Committee, and 11 leading members of various democratic parties. From 1966 to 1970, Jiang Qing at various meetings named 24 Members and Alternate Members of the Eighth C.P.C. Central Committee and hurled false charges at them, so that they were persecuted one after another. After Jiang Qing named and made false accusations against Zhang Linzhi, Minister of the Coal Industry, he was illegally incarcerated and subsequently died of serious injuries from beating.

The Lin Biao and Jiang Qing counter-revolutionary cliques framed and persecuted large numbers of officers of the Chinese People's Liberation Army in an attempt to put it under their complete control. On July 25, 1967, Lin Biao called for the "thorough smashing of the P.L.A. General Political Department." Huang Yongsheng, Wu Faxian, Li Zuopeng and Qiu Huizuo respectively framed and persecuted large numbers of officers in the Headquarters of the General Staff, the General Political Department, the General Logistics Department, the Air Force and the Navy of the Chinese People's Liberation Army. The Lin Biao and Jiang Qing counter-revolutionary cliques cooked up so many false cases in the Chinese People's Liberation Army that over 80,000 people were framed and persecuted, of whom 1,169 died under persecution.

The Lin Biao and Jiang Qing counter-revolutionary cliques framed and persecuted Party and government leaders at various levels in an attempt to seize departmental and regional leadership that they had not yet got hold of. In January of 1968, Kang Sheng and others framed cadres in the Organization Department of the C.P.C. Central Committee and directly controlled leadership in that department. The Lin Biao and Jiang Qing counter-revolutionary cliques framed and persecuted large numbers of cadres and people's policemen in people's public security organs, people's procuratorates and people's courts at various levels, of whom 1,565 were hounded to death. The Lin Biao and Jiang Qing counter-revolutionary cliques framed and persecuted large numbers of cadres in various provinces, autonomous regions and municipalities directly under the central government. Under the instruction and instigation of Kang Sheng, Xie Fuzhi and others, leadership of Beijing municipality was seized and 13 of its leading cadres were framed and persecuted. Liu Ren and Deng Tuo, secretaries of the municipal Party committee, and Vice-Mayors Wu Han and Yue Songsheng, were persecuted to death. Leadership of Shanghai municipality was seized and 12 of its leading cadres were framed and persecuted as a result of the instruction and instigation of Zhang Chunqiao and Yao Wenyuan. Mayor Cao Diqiu and Vice-Mayor Jin Zhonghua died from persecution. In 1967 and 1968, Zhang Chunqiao directly manipulated and ordered the "You Xuetao group" in Shanghai to undertake such special tasks of espionage as tailing, shadowing, kidnapping, ransacking people's homes, taking people into custody, extorting confessions by torture, and fabricating intelligence. The group trumped up false cases, framed and persecuted cadres and ordinary people, and falsely charged leading cadres in east China with "organizing an underground armed detachment south of the Changjiang (Yangtze) River" and "plotting a mutiny."

The Lin Biao and Jiang Qing counter-revolutionary cliques created large numbers of false cases, incited beating, smashing and looting throughout the country, and persecuted large numbers of cadres and ordinary people. In 1967, Kang Sheng and others trumped up the case of a "Xinjiang renegade clique." In 1967 and 1968, Huang Yongsheng and company concocted, one after another, the case of a "Guangdong underground Party organization" and that of a "counter-revolutionary clique" in the P.L.A. Guangzhou Units. Under Chen Boda's instigation, a false case in eastern Hebei Province brought serious consequences with a large number of cadres and ordinary people persecuted in 1967. Kang Sheng and Xie Fuzhi rigged up the case of "enemy agent Zhao Jianmin" in Yunnan in 1968. In the same year, because of the agitation of Kang Sheng and Xie Fuzhi, the false case of an "Inner Mongolian people's revolutionary party" entailed disastrous consequences, with large numbers of cadres and ordinary people persecuted or hounded to death or disability. Between 1967 and 1969, the case of a "counter-revolutionary 'northeast gang' that betrayed the Party and capitulated to the enemy" was trumped up under the agitation of the Lin Biao and Jiang Qing counter-revolutionary cliques. In October of 1966, Jiang Qing collaborated with Ye Qun in ordering Jiang Tengjiao to carry out an unlawful search in Shanghai of the homes of Zheng Junli, Zhao Dan, Gu Eryi, Tong Zhiling and Chen Liting, who were later persecuted physically. False cases concocted under the instruction and instigation of the Lin Biao and Jiang Qing counter-revolutionary cliques led to the framing and persecution of large numbers of cadres and ordinary members of Communist Party, government and army organs at various levels and various democratic parties and people's organizations, cadres and other people in various circles and returned overseas Chinese. Among those well-known figures in various circles who were persecuted to death were: noted writers and artists including Lao She, Zhao Shuli, Zhou Xinfang, Gai Jiaotian, Pan Tianshou, Ying Yunwei, Zheng Junli and Sun Weishi; noted professors including Xiong Qinglai, Jian Bozan, He Sijing, Wang Shourong, Gu Yuzhen, Li Guangtian, Rao Yutai, Liu Pansui and Ma Te; noted scientists including Zhao Jiuzhang, Ye Zhupei, Zhang Zongsui, Liu Chongle, Chen Huanyong and Zhou Ren; famous medical specialists including Hu Zhengxiang, Zhang Changshao, Ji Suhua, Lu Shouyan, Ye Xichun and Li Zhongren; outstanding sports coaches including Fu Qifang, Rong Guotuan and Jiang Yongning; well-known model workers including Meng Tai and Shi Chuanxiang; and well-known figures in overseas Chinese affairs including Fang Fang, Xu Li, Huang Jie, Chen Xujing, Huang Qinshu and Chen Manyun. The Lin Biao and Jiang Qing counter-revolutionary cliques seriously disrupted national unity and had large numbers of cadres and ordinary people of various minority nationalities cruelly persecuted. As a result, Jiyatai and others were persecuted to death.

The Lin Biao and Jiang Qing counter-revolutionary cliques instigated large-scale incidents of violence among mass organizations throughout the country, attempting thus to seize power and cruelly suppress the people. At the instigation of Zhang Chunqiao, an armed clash, known as the Kangping Road Incident, was triggered in Shanghai on December 28, 1966, resulting in 91 injured and setting a vile precedent for seizing power by instigating violent incidents throughout the country. With the support of Zhang Chunqiao and Yao Wenyuan, Wang Xiaoyu, then chairman of the Shandong Provincial Revolutionary Committee, engineered in May of 1967 a violent incident in the compound of the provincial revolutionary committee in Ji'nan, resulting in 388 persons arrested and imprisoned. On August 4 of the same year, Wang Hongwen organized and directed people to surround and attack the Shanghai Diesel Engine Plant, resulting in 650 people imprisoned, injured or maimed.

The Lin Biao and Jiang Qing counter-revolutionary cliques each plotted to seize supreme Party and state power for itself. While they formed an alliance, their sharp contradictions remained. In 1969, Lin Biao was designated successor to Chairman Mao Zedong. In 1970, Lin Biao realized that the forces of Jiang Qing, Zhang Chunqiao and company were growing in such a manner as to surpass his own, so he plotted to "take over" the leadership ahead of schedule. While well aware that Jiang Qing could never succeed in her ambitions, Lin Biao knew that it was impossible for Chairman Mao Zedong to support his "takeover" in advance. Therefore, in September of 1971, the Lin Biao counter-revolutionary clique decided to cast off its mask and stage an armed coup and assassinate Chairman Mao Zedong. As early as October of 1969, Wu Faxian, commander of the Air Force, turned over to Lin Liguo all power to place the Air Force under his command and at his disposal. In October of 1970, Lin Liguo organized a secret backbone force for the armed coup, which he named the "joint fleet." In March of 1971, Lin Liguo, Zhou Yuchi and others mapped out in Shanghai a plan for the armed coup, which they named *Outline of "Project 571."* In line with the plan for establishing a "command team" as described in the *Outline*, Lin Liguo summoned Jiang Tengjiao and Wang Weiguo, political commissar of the P.L.A. Unit 7341, Chen Liyun, political commissar of the P.L.A. Unit 7350, and Zhou Jianping, deputy commander of the Air Force of the P.L.A. Nanjing Units, to a secret meeting in Shanghai on March 31, at which Jiang Tengjiao was put in charge of liaison between the three places of Nanjing, Shanghai and Hangzhou with a view to co-ordination and concerted operation. On September 5 and 6 of the same year, after receiving secret reports first from Zhou Yuchi and then from Huang Yongsheng about Chairman Mao Zedong's talks which showed that he was aware of Lin Biao's scheme to seize power, Lin Biao and Ye Qun decided to take action to assassinate Chairman Mao Zedong on his inspection tour and stage an armed coup. On September 8, Lin Biao issued the following hand-written order for the armed coup: "Expect you to act according to the order transmitted by Comrades Liguo and Yuchi." Lin Liguo and Zhou Yuchi then gave detailed assignments to Jiang Tengjiao and Wang Fei, deputy chief-of-staff of the Air Force Headquarters, and other key members of the "joint fleet." While the Lin Biao counter-revolutionary clique was plotting intensively for the armed coup, Chairman Mao Zedong, having been alerted by their plot, suddenly changed his itinerary and safely returned to Beijing on September 12.

After the failure of their plan for the assassination, Lin Biao then made preparations for fleeing south with Huang

Yongsheng, Wu Faxian, Li Zuopeng and Qiu Huizuo to Guangzhou, the base where he was prepared to stage the armed coup, in an attempt to set up a separate central government there and split the state. At Lin Biao's order, Hu Ping, deputy chief-of-staff of the Air Force Headquarters, had eight planes ready for the flight south to Guangzhou. On September 12, he secretly dispatched the special plane, No. 256, to Shanhaiguan for the use of Lin Biao, Ye Qun and Lin Liguo, who were then in Beidaihe. At a few minutes past 10 o'clock that evening, Premier Zhou Enlai inquired about the unexpected dispatch of the special plane, No. 256, to Shanhaiguan and ordered that it be brought back to Beijing at once. Hu Ping lied, saying that the special plane, No. 256, had gone to Shanhaiguan on a training flight and had developed engine trouble, refusing to carry out the order for bringing it back to Beijing. Meanwhile, he reported to Zhou Yuchi that the Premier had inquired about the movement of the plane. Zhou Yuchi in turn reported this to Lin Liguo. While issuing directives to those in charge of the Navy Aviation Corps' Shanhaiguan Airport, first at 23:35 hours on September 12 and then at 00:06 hours on September 13, Li Zuopeng distorted Premier Zhou Enlai's directive that the special plane, No. 256, "Cannot take off without a joint order from four persons," namely, Zhou Enlai, Huang Yongsheng, Wu Faxian and Li Zuopeng, saying, "The plane must not be allowed to take off unless one of the four leading officials gives the order." At 00:20 hours on September 13, when Pan Hao, director of the Navy Aviation Corps' Shanhaiguan Airport, who had discovered the abnormal situation at the time, phoned Li Zuopeng, asking what they should do if the plane were to take off forcibly, Li Zuopeng still did not take any measure to prevent the plane from taking off, thus enabling Lin Biao, Ye Qun and Lin Liguo to defect by the special plane, No. 256. Learning that Premier Zhou Enlai had inquired about the special plane's flight to Shanhaiguan, Lin Biao decided it was impossible to carry out the plan of fleeing south to Guangzhou and setting up a separate government there. So they boarded the plane and took off forcibly at 00:32 hours on September 13 to flee abroad in defection. The plane crashed on the way, killing all those aboard.

After learning about Lin Biao's defection, Zhou Yuchi and others seized the helicopter, No. 3685, in Beijing and took off at 03:15 hours on September 13 to flee the country, but the helicopter was forced to land. Large amounts of confidential state documents stolen by the Lin Biao counter-revolutionary clique and its plans for an armed coup were captured from the helicopter.

After Lin Biao and others died on their flight abroad, the Jiang Qing counter-revolutionary clique, in an attempt to seize Party and state leadership, carried on criminal activities to frame and persecute leading members at various levels. From 1974 to 1976, the Jiang Qing counter-revolutionary clique instructed writing groups such as "Liang Xiao," "Chi Heng" and "Luo Siding" to carry out counter-revolutionary agitation for vilifying leading cadres at various levels who had just returned to their posts as "having turned from bourgeois democrats to capitalist-roaders," thus becoming targets of their so-called continued revolution. In 1976, Jiang Qing, Zhang Chunqiao, Yao Wenyuan and Wang Hongwen created new disturbances throughout the country and framed and persecuted large numbers of leading cadres with the ultimate objective of subverting the government. In March Jiang Qing, in a talk with leading members from 12 provinces and autonomous regions, named a number of leading cadres at central and local levels and hurled false charges at them. In the same year, Zhang Chunqiao instigated Ma Tianshui and Xu Jingxian, vice-chairmen of the Shanghai Municipal Revolutionary Committee, to speak at a meeting attended by more than 10,000 people in Shanghai and vilify leading cadres who had resumed work as "turning from bourgeois democrats to capitalist-roaders." In the same year, Wang Hongwen and Yao Wenyuan ordered Lu Ying, editor-in-chief of *Renmin Ribao* (*People's Daily*), to dispatch people to some departments of the State Council and some provinces to cook up materials according to their intentions for framing veteran cadres who had resumed work as "having organized landlords' restitution corps" and "trying to reverse correct verdicts and stage a comeback." They used the materials to justify their seizure of power from those departments and regions which were not yet under their control. From March to May of 1976, the Jiang Qing counter-revolutionary clique made up stories, slandering ordinary people in Nanjing, Beijing and other places who honoured the memory of Premier Zhou Enlai as "counter-revolutionaries." The clique also vilified Vice-Premier Deng Xiaoping as "the chief boss behind the counter-revolutionary political incident" at Tian An Men Square and agitated for large-scale suppression and persecution of cadres and ordinary people.

Zhang Chunqiao and Wang Hongwen, principal culprits in the case of the Jiang Qing counter-revolutionary clique, made Shanghai their base for building and expanding a "militia force" under their direct control. As early as August of 1967, a report cleared by Zhang Chunqiao, entitled "plans of the Shanghai Municipal Revolutionary Committee for setting up the 'verbal attack and armed defence' headquarters," called for "using the gun to protect revolution made with the pen" and for vigorously building up armed forces under their control. From 1973 to 1976, Wang Hongwen said on many occasions to Ma Tianshui, Xu Jingxian and Wang Xiuzhen, key members of the Jiang Qing counter-revolutionary clique in Shanghai, that "the army must not be allowed to lead the militia," that "it's Chunqiao and me who organized the people's militia in Shanghai," that "you must run it well for me," that "what worries me most is that the army is not in our hands," and that "we must be prepared for guerrilla warfare," urging them to step up the expansion of the "militia force." The Jiang Qing counter-revolutionary clique planned to use this armed force which they regarded as their own to engineer an armed rebellion in Shanghai. In August of 1976, Ding Sheng, a remaining confederate of the Lin Biao clique who had thrown his lot with the Jiang Qing counter-revolutionary clique and commander of the P.L.A. Nanjing Units at the time, arrived in Shanghai. He told Ma Tianshui, Xu Jingxian and Wang Xiuzhen, "My biggest worry is Unit 6453" stationed near Shanghai, that "I have no control over it" and that "you must be prepared for any eventuality." Ma Tianshui then made a decision and 74,220 rifles, 300 artillery pieces and more than 10 million rounds of ammunition were issued from a munitions depot under their control to the "militia." On September 21, after being briefed in Beijing by Xu Jingxian about Ding Sheng's talk and about the hand-out of weapons to the "militia," Zhang Chunqiao said to Xu Jingxian: "Keep your eyes open for new trends in the class struggle." On September 23, Wang Hongwen made a telephone call to Wang Xiuzhen, saying: "Be on your guard, for the struggle isn't over yet. The bourgeoisie inside the Party will not be reconciled to defeat." On October 8, after learning that Jiang Qing, Zhang Chunqiao, Yao Wenyuan and Wang Hongwen had been taken into custody, Xu Jingxian, Wang Xiuzhen and others decided to stage an armed rebellion. The command teams they had organized for the armed rebellion then moved into their command posts, and 15 transmitter-receivers were installed to link them up by telecommunications. They also assembled and deployed 33,500 "militiamen." On October 9, Shi Shangying, who was in charge of the Shanghai militia headquarters, ordered that the "militia" be concentrated with over 27,000 guns and artillery pieces of various types. On October 12, Zhong Dingdong, another member in charge of the Shanghai militia headquarters, drew up two specific operation plans, code named "Han No. 1" and "Fang No. 2." On the evening of the same day, Wang Shaoyong, vice-chairman of the Shanghai Municipal Revolutionary Committee, Zhu Yongjia, leading member of the Shanghai writing group, Chen Ada, leading member of the industrial and communication group of the Shanghai Municipal Revolutionary Committee, and others met to plan production stoppages, strikes, parades and demonstrations. They put forward the counter-revolutionary slogans "Return Jiang Qing to us," "Return Chunqiao to us," "Return Wenyuan to us" and "Return Hongwen to us," readying themselves for "a life-and-death struggle." Thanks to the powerful measures adopted by the Party Central Committee and the struggle waged by the people of Shanghai, their scheme for an armed coup failed to materialize.

This court has held a total of 42 sessions for investigation and debate, during which 49 witnesses and victims appeared in court to testify, and 873 pieces of evidence were examined. The above-mentioned offences committed by the Lin Biao and Jiang Qing counter-revolutionary cliques have been verified by great amounts of material and documentary evidence, conclusions of expert corroboration, testimonies of witnesses and statements of victims. The facts are clear and the evidence conclusive.

Criminal Liability of the Ten Principal Culprits

Since Lin Biao, Kang Sheng, Xie Fuzhi, Ye Qun, Lin Liguo and Zhou Yuchi, who were among the 16 principal culprits in the case of the Lin Biao and Jiang Qing counter-revolutionary cliques, are dead, the Special Procuratorate Under the Supreme People's Procuratorate has decided not to pursue their criminal liability, in accordance with Article 11 of the Law of Criminal Procedure of the People's Republic of China. The Special Procuratorate also decides that except Jiang Qing and the other nine principal culprits, the other defendants in the case will be dealt with separately according to law. Following are the offences committed by Jiang Qing, Zhang Chunqiao, Yao Wenyuan, Wang Hongwen, Chen Boda, Huang Yongsheng, Wu Faxian, Li Zuopeng, Qiu Huizuo and Jiang Tengjiao, for which they should be held criminally liable as confirmed by this court:

(1) The defendant, Jiang Qing, who acted as a ringleader in organizing and leading a counter-revolutionary clique for the purpose of overthrowing the people's democratic dictatorship, was a principal culprit in the case of the counter-revolutionary clique. Jiang Qing framed and persecuted Liu Shaoqi, Chairman of the People's Republic of China. Working in collaboration with Kang Sheng and Chen Boda, she decided in July of 1967 to have Liu Shaoqi persecuted physically and hence deprived of the freedom of action. From May of 1967, Jiang Qing assumed direct control of the "group for inquiring into the special case of Liu Shaoqi and Wang Guangmei" and, in collusion with Kang Sheng and Xie Fuzhi, ordered the group to extort confessions from those arrested and put in custody, concoct false evidence and frame Liu Shaoqi as a "renegade," "enemy agent" and "counter-revolutionary." In order to rig up false evidence and persecute Liu Shaoqi, Jiang Qing made the decision in 1967 to arrest and imprison Yang Yichen, Yang Chengzuo, Wang Guangen, Hao Miao and seven others. When Yang Chengzuo was critically ill, Jiang Qing decided to "step up the interrogation" of him. As a result, Yang Chengzuo was persecuted to death. The special case group under Jiang Qing's direction also had Wang Guangen persecuted to death. In collusion with Xie Fuzhi, Jiang Qing ordered that repeated actions be taken to extort confessions from Zhang Zhongyi who was critically ill. As a result, he died just two hours after an interrogation. In collaboration with Kang Sheng, Xie Fuzhi and others, Jiang Qing instructed the special case group to extract confessions from Ding Juequn and Meng Yongqian and rig up false evidence for framing Liu Shaoqi as a "renegade." As a result of the false charges made by Jiang Qing and others, Liu Shaoqi was imprisoned and persecuted to death.

On July 21, 1968, Jiang Qing worked hand in glove with Kang Sheng in cooking up such false charges as "renegade," "enemy agent" or "element having illicit relations with foreign countries" against 88 Members and Alternate Members of the Eighth Central Committee of the Communist Party of China.

From 1966 to 1970, Jiang Qing named 24 Members and Alternate Members of the Eighth C.P.C. Central Committee and hurled false charges at them at various meetings. As a result, they were persecuted one after another.

On December 14, 1966, Jiang Qing attacked Zhang Linzhi (Minister of the Coal Industry — Ed.) by name on false charges. As a result, Zhang Linzhi was illegally incarcerated and beaten up, and he later died from serious wounds. On December 27 of the same year, Jiang Qing smeared Shi Chuanxiang, a national model worker and a night-soil collector in Beijing, as a "scab." Shi Chuanxiang thus suffered serious maltreatment and later died from torment.

In October of 1966, Jiang Qing collaborated with Ye Qun in ordering Jiang Tengjiao to search and ransack the homes of Zheng Junli and four other persons in Shanghai, which was against the law. As a result, they were persecuted physically.

In 1976, Jiang Qing worked hand in glove with Zhang Chunqiao, Yao Wenyuan and Wang Hongwen to create new disturbances across the country. In a talk to leading members of 12 provinces and autonomous regions in March of the same year, Jiang Qing attacked a number of central and local leading cadres by name on false charges.

Jiang Qing was a ringleader of the Lin Biao and Jiang Qing counter-revolutionary cliques. She bore direct or indirect responsibilities for all the offences, committed during the decade of turmoil by the counter-revolutionary clique she organized and led, of endangering the People's Republic of China, working to overthrow the government and tyrannizing the people.

The defendant, Jiang Qing, has been found guilty of organizing and leading a counter-revolutionary clique as provided in Article 98 of the Criminal Law of the People's Republic of China, of plotting to overthrow the government as provided in Article 92, of conducting propaganda and agitation for counter-revolutionary purposes as provided in Article 102, and of framing and persecuting people as provided in Article 138. She caused particularly grave harm to the state and the people in a particularly flagrant way.

(2)   The defendant, Zhang Chunqiao, who collaborated with Jiang Qing in organizing and leading a counter-revolutionary clique for the purpose of overthrowing the people's democratic dictatorship, was a principal culprit in the case of the counter-revolutionary clique. As the initiator and an all-time instigator and plotter in seizing power from the people's democratic political power during the decade of turmoil, he caused extremely grave harm to the state and the people.

In January of 1967, Zhang Chunqiao said: "We must seize power everywhere." From 1967 to 1975, he said on many occasions that "the great cultural revolution" meant "a change of dynasty." He worked hand in glove with Jiang Qing in leading their counter-revolutionary clique in a great deal of activities aimed at usurping Party and state leadership.

In order to seize leadership of Shanghai municipality, Zhang Chunqiao triggered off an armed clash in Shanghai on December 28, 1966, known as the Kangping Road Incident, which resulted in 91 injured. In May of 1967, he supported Wang Xiaoyu to engineer a violent incident in Jinan, which resulted in 388 persons arrested and imprisoned.

In December of 1966, Zhang Chunqiao summoned Kuai Dafu alone and instructed him to organize a demonstration and agitate for "overthrowing Liu Shaoqi" for the first time in society at large.

Leadership of Shanghai municipality was seized under Zhang Chunqiao's instruction and instigation. Twelve leading cadres of the municipality were labelled "renegades," "enemy agents" or "counter-revolutionaries." Cao Diqiu and Jin Zhonghua were persecuted to death.

Controlled and directed by Zhang Chunqiao, the "You Xuetao group" carried out special tasks of espionage, trumped up cases to persecute cadres and other people, and falsely charged leading cadres in east China with "organizing an underground armed detachment south of the Changjiang (Yangtze) River" and "plotting a mutiny."

In 1976, Zhang Chunqiao collaborated with Jiang Qing, Yao Wenyuan and Wang Hongwen in creating new disturbances across the country. In March of the same year, Zhang Chunqiao instructed Ma Tianshui and Xu Jingxian to smear, at a mass meeting of 10,000 people in Shanghai, those leading cadres who had resumed work as having turned "from bourgeois democrats into cap-italic-roaders" and become targets of what they called continued revolution.

Zhang Chunqiao, in collusion with Wang Hongwen and others, made Shanghai their base for building up a "militia force" under their direct control, and plotted an armed rebellion there.

The defendant, Zhang Chunqiao, has been found guilty of organizing and leading a counter-revolutionary clique as provided in Article 98 of the Criminal Law of the People's Republic of China, of scheming to overthrow the government as provided in Article 92, of plotting an armed rebellion as provided in Article 93, of conducting propaganda and agitation for counter-revolutionary purposes as provided in Article 102, and of framing and persecuting people as provided in Article 138. He caused particularly grave harm to the state and the people in a particularly flagrant way.

(3) The defendant, Yao Wenyuan, who organized and led a counter-revolutionary clique for the purpose of overthrowing the people's democratic dictatorship, was a principal culprit in the case of the counter-revolutionary clique. He took an active part in Jiang Qing's activities to seize supreme power.

Yao Wenyuan directly controlled the mass media and conducted propaganda and agitation for counter-revolutionary ends over a long period. From 1974 to 1976, he instructed writing groups including "Liang Xiao," "Chi Heng" and "Luo Siding" to vilify leading cadres at various levels who had resumed work, accusing them of having turned "from bourgeois democrats into capitalist-roaders" and become targets of the so-called continued revolution, thus agitating for framing and persecuting them.

In 1967, Yao Wenyuan took an active part in seizing leadership of Shanghai municipality. He joined in framing leading cadres of the municipality including Cao Diqiu.

Yao Wenyuan was one of those who supported Wang

Xiaoyu's plan to engineer a violent incident in Jinan in May of 1967.

In 1976, Yao Wenyuan collaborated with Jiang Qing, Zhang Chunqiao and Wang Hongwen in creating new disturbances across the country. From January to September of the same year, he instructed Lu Ying to dispatch people to some departments of the State Council and some provinces to fabricate materials according to their intentions so as to frame those leading cadres who had resumed work. From March to May of the same year, Yao Wenyuan, by trumping up charges, smeared people in Nanjing, Beijing and other places who mourned the death of Premier Zhou Enlai as "counter-revolutionaries," falsely charged Deng Xiaoping with being the "chief boss behind the counter-revolutionary political incident" at Tian An Men Square, and agitated for suppressing and persecuting large numbers of cadres and ordinary people.

The defendant, Yao Wenyuan, has been found guilty of organizing and leading a counter-revolutionary clique as provided in Article 98 of the Criminal Law of the People's Republic of China, of plotting to overthrow the government as provided in Article 92, of conducting propaganda and agitation for counter-revolutionary ends as provided in Article 102, and of framing and persecuting people as provided in Article 138.

(4) **The defendant, Wang Hongwen, who organized and led a counter-revolutionary clique for the purpose of overthrowing the people's democratic dictatorship, was a principal culprit in the case of the counter-revolutionary clique.** He took an active part in Jiang Qing's activities to seize supreme power.

On December 28, 1966, Wang Hongwen participated in triggering off the Kangping Road Incident of violence, which resulted in 91 injured. On August 4, 1967, he organized and directed people to surround and attack the

Shanghai Diesel Engine Plant, and 650 people were imprisoned, wounded or maimed.

In 1976, Wang Hongwen collaborated with Jiang Qing, Zhang Chunqiao and Yao Wenyuan in creating new disturbances across the country. He instructed Lu Ying to dispatch people to a number of provinces to fabricate materials according to their intentions for framing leading cadres who had resumed work.

Working in collusion with Zhang Chunqiao, Wang Hongwen made Shanghai their base for building up a "militia force" under their direct control. He instructed Ma Tianshui, Xu Jingxian and Wang Xiuzhen time and again to step up the expansion of the "militia force," and plotted an armed rebellion in Shanghai.

The defendant, Wang Hongwen, has been found guilty of organizing and leading a counter-revolutionary clique as provided in Article 98 of the Criminal Law of the People's Republic of China, of conspiring to overthrow the government as provided in Article 92, of instigating an armed rebellion as provided in Article 93, of causing injury to people for counter-revolutionary purposes as provided in Article 101, and of framing and persecuting people as provided in Article 138.

(5) The defendant, Chen Boda, who played an active part in a counter-revolutionary clique for the purpose of overthrowing the people's democratic dictatorship, was a principal culprit in the case of the counter-revolutionary clique. He took an active part in the activities of Lin Biao and Jiang Qing to seize supreme power.

Chen Boda controlled the mass media and conducted propaganda and agitation for counter-revolutionary purposes. In 1966, he raised such slogans as "sweep away all monsters and demons" and whipped up extensive framing and persecution of cadres and ordinary people.

In July of 1967, Chen Boda collaborated with Jiang Qing and Kang Sheng in deciding to have Liu Shaoqi persecuted physically and deprived of his freedom of action ever since.

From late 1966 to 1968, Chen Boda on quite a few occasions smeared Lu Dingyi, Vice-Premier of the State Council, as an "active counter-revolutionary," "renegade" and "hidden traitor," and decided to have his health ruined.

In December of 1967, Chen Boda said in Tangshan that the C.P.C. organization in eastern Hebei Province "was probably a party of Kuomintang-Communist co-operation, and in fact it might be the Kuomintang members, or renegades, who were playing a dominant role here." A case was thus trumped up at his instigation, which brought serious consequences, with many cadres and ordinary people in eastern Hebei persecuted.

The defendant, Chen Boda, has been found guilty of actively joining a counter-revolutionary clique as provided in Article 98 of the Criminal Law of the People's Republic of China, of conspiring to overthrow the government as provided in Article 92, of conducting propaganda and agitation for counter-revolutionary purposes as provided in Article 102, and of framing and persecuting people as provided in Article 138.

(6) The defendant, Huang Yongsheng, who organized and led a counter-revolutionary clique for the purpose of overthrowing the people's democratic dictatorship, was a principal culprit in the case of the counter-revolutionary clique. He actively participated in Lin Biao's activities to seize supreme power.

On November 3, 1970, Huang Yongsheng agreed to the proposal raised by the group in charge of the special case of Peng Dehuai that "Peng Dehuai be dismissed from all posts inside and outside the Party, expelled from the Party for good, sentenced to life imprisonment and deprived of civil rights for life." As a result, Peng Dehuai was subsequently persecuted.

In June of 1967, Huang Yongsheng approved the "report for instruction on investigation for the purpose of rounding up renegades," which was submitted by the head of the military control commission stationed in the Guangzhou Municipal Public Security Bureau, and its appendix, "plan for investigation, No. 1," scheming to frame Ye Jianying as a "renegade." In June of 1968, he turned over to Ye Qun materials falsely charging Ye Jianying with "plotting a counter-revolutionary coup."

In 1968, Huang Yongsheng, in collaboration with Wu Faxian, fabricated charges against Luo Ruiqing, smearing him as a "counter-revolutionary who has committed heinous crimes." Huang Yongsheng also framed leading cadres in the Headquarters of the P.L.A. General Staff. In December of the same year, he slandered the P.L.A. General Political Department as "recruiting renegades" and took an active part in Lin Biao's criminal activities for the "thorough smashing of the P.L.A. General Political Department."

From October of 1967 to March of 1968, Huang Yongsheng proposed to investigate the history of the underground C.P.C. organization in Guangdong Province before liberation and decided to examine the records of Wen Niansheng, Deputy Commander of the P.L.A. Guangzhou Units, and others. This gave rise to the false cases of the "Guangdong underground Party organization" and a "counter-revolutionary clique" in the P.L.A. Guangzhou Units. As a result, large numbers of cadres and ordinary people were framed and persecuted, and the Vice-Governor of Guangdong, Lin Qiangyun, and Wen Niansheng were persecuted to death.

On September 6, 1971, Huang Yongsheng secretly informed Lin Biao of Chairman Mao Zedong's talks which showed he was aware that Lin Biao was conspiring to seize power. This prompted Lin Biao's decision to take action to assassinate Chairman Mao Zedong and engineer an armed coup d'etat.

The defendant, Huang Yongsheng, has been found guilty of organizing and leading a counter-revolutionary clique as provided in Article 98 of the Criminal Law of the People's Republic of China, of conspiring to overthrow the government as provided in Article 92, and of framing and persecuting people as provided in Article 138.

(7) The defendant, Wu Faxian, who organized and led a counter-revolutionary clique for the purpose of overthrowing the people's democratic dictatorship, was a principal culprit in the case of the counter-revolutionary clique. He actively participated in Lin Biao's activities to seize supreme power.

Receiving Lin Biao's instructions in August of 1966, Wu Faxian had materials prepared on September 3, accusing He Long of plotting to seize leadership in the Air Force, and sent them to Lin Biao. In August of 1968, Wu Faxian, in collaboration with Huang Yongsheng, fabricated charges against Luo Ruiqing, smearing him as a "counter-revolutionary who has committed heinous crimes."

Wu Faxian laid false charges against a number of leading cadres in the Air Force, alleging that they attempted to "seize power." He approved the detention and persecution of 174 cadres and rank-and-filers in the Air Force, among whom Gu Qian, Chief of Staff of the Air Force Command of the P.L.A. Nanjing Units, and Liu Shanben, deputy superintendent of the Air Force Academy, were persecuted to death.

In October of 1969, Wu Faxian turned over to Lin Liguo all power to place the Air Force under his command and at his disposal, thus enabling him to form a "joint fleet," which constituted the backbone force in the plot of the Lin Biao counter-revolutionary clique to assassinate Chairman Mao Zedong and stage an armed coup d'etat.

The defendant, Wu Faxian, has been found guilty of organizing and leading a counter-revolutionary clique as provided in Article 98 of the Criminal Law of the People's Republic of China, of conspiring to overthrow the government as provided in Article 92, and of persecuting people on false charges as provided in Article 138.

(8) **The defendant, Li Zuopeng, who organized and led a counter-revolutionary clique for the purpose of overthrowing the people's democratic dictatorship, was a principal culprit in the case of the counter-revolutionary clique.** Li Zuopeng took an active part in Lin Biao's activities to seize supreme power.

In April of 1968, he falsely accused He Long and others of trying to "usurp army leadership and oppose the Party." He attacked 120 cadres in the Navy by name on false charges.

At 11:35 p.m. on September 12 and at 00:06 a.m. on September 13, 1971, Li Zuopeng twice distorted Premier Zhou Enlai's directive just before the defection of Lin Biao and Ye Qun. When Pan Hao, director of the Navy Aviation Corps' Shanhaiguan Airport, in an emergency phone call at 00:20 a.m. on September 13, asked for instruction on what he should do if the plane were to take off forcibly, Li Zuopeng did not take any measure to prevent the takeoff, thus allowing Lin Biao to escape abroad by air. Afterwards, Li Zuopeng tried to cover up his crime by altering the logbook entry of the relevant phone calls.

The defendant, Li Zuopeng, has been found guilty of organizing and leading a counter-revolutionary clique as provided in Article 98 of the Criminal Law of the People's Republic of China, of conspiring to overthrow the government as provided in Article 92, and of framing and persecuting people as provided in Article 138.

(9) **The defendant, Qiu Huizuo, who organized and led a counter-revolutionary clique for the purpose of overthrowing the people's democratic dictatorship, was a**

principal culprit in the case of the counter-revolutionary clique. Qiu Huizuo took an active part in Lin Biao's activities to seize supreme power.

In 1967, Qiu Huizuo instructed some persons to steal the archives of the P.L.A. General Political Department and framed cadres in the department. He played an important role in Lin Biao's criminal activities of "smashing the General Political Department."

Between 1967 and 1971, Qiu Huizuo set up a kangaroo court in the P.L.A. General Logistics Department to extort confessions through torture, and directly framed and persecuted 462 cadres and ordinary people, among whom Tang Ping, Zhou Changgeng, Gu Zizhuang, Zhang Shusen, Shen Maoxing, Wang Shuchen, Zhang Lingdou and Hua Diping were persecuted to death.

The defendant, Qiu Huizuo, has been found guilty of organizing and leading a counter-revolutionary clique as provided in Article 98 of the Criminal Law of the People's Republic of China, of conspiring to overthrow the government as provided in Article 92, and of framing and persecuting people as provided in Article 138.

(10) The defendant, Jiang Tengjiao, who played an active role in the counter-revolutionary clique for the purpose of overthrowing the people's democratic dictatorship, was a principal culprit in the case of the counter-revolutionary clique. On March 31, 1971, Jiang Tengjiao attended a secret meeting called by Lin Liguo in Shanghai to establish a "command team" for an armed coup, at which he was made the person responsible for liaison between the three places of Nanjing, Shanghai and Hangzhou "with a view to co-ordination and concerted operation." Having received, via Lin Liguo, a hand-written order from Lin Biao on September 8 for an armed coup, Jiang Tengjiao took part in working out the details for assassinating Chairman Mao Zedong, and assumed the position of first-line commander for action in the Shanghai

area. Following the failure of the plot to murder Chairman Mao Zedong, Jiang Tengjiao took an active part in the counter-revolutionary action of Lin Biao and Ye Qun in preparing for fleeing south to Guangzhou.

The defendant, Jiang Tengjiao, has been found guilty of playing an active role in a counter-revolutionary clique as provided in Article 98 of the Criminal Law of the People's Republic of China, of instigating an armed rebellion as provided in Article 93, and of attempting to kill people for counter-revolutionary purposes as provided in Article 101.

Among the above-mentioned defendants, Wang Hongwen, Chen Boda, Wu Faxian, Li Zuopeng, Qiu Huizuo and Jiang Tengjiao each gave an account of the offences he had committed. Jiang Tengjiao confessed his offences the day after Lin Biao's defection. Wu Faxian, Qiu Huizuo and Jiang Tengjiao exposed crimes committed by Lin Biao, Jiang Qing and other co-defendants in the case. Huang Yongsheng confessed some of his offences. Yao Wenyuan described his offences as mistakes and denied that they were crimes. Zhang Chunqiao refused to answer the questions put to him by the bench. Jiang Qing disrupted order in court.

Judgement on the Defendants According to Criminal Law

In view of the facts, nature and degree of the offences Jiang Qing and the other nine defendants committed and the damage they did to society, and in accordance with Articles 90, 92, 93, 98, 101, 102, 103 and 138, as well as Articles 20, 43, 52, 53 and 64, of the Criminal Law of the People's Republic of China, this court now passes the following judgement:

Jiang Qing is sentenced to death with a two-year reprieve and permanent deprivation of political rights;

Zhang Chunqiao is sentenced to death with a two-year reprieve and permanent deprivation of political rights;

Yao Wenyuan is sentenced to 20 years' imprisonment and deprivation of political rights for five years;

Wang Hongwen is sentenced to life imprisonment and permanent deprivation of political rights;

Chen Boda is sentenced to 18 years' imprisonment and deprivation of political rights for five years;

Huang Yongsheng is sentenced to 18 years' imprisonment and deprivation of political rights for five years;

Wu Faxian is sentenced to 17 years' imprisonment and deprivation of political rights for five years;

Li Zuopeng is sentenced to 17 years' imprisonment and deprivation of political rights for five years;

Qiu Huizuo is sentenced to 16 years' imprisonment and deprivation of political rights for five years;

Jiang Tengjiao is sentenced to 18 years' imprisonment and deprivation of political rights for five years.

The fixed terms of imprisonment for those listed above who are sentenced to such a penalty shall run from the first day of enforcement of the sentences. Where an offender has been held in prior custody, the duration of such custody shall be deducted from the term of imprisonment at the rate of one day for each day spent in prior custody.

This judgement is final.

January 23, 1981

The Special Court under the Supreme People's Court of the People's Republic of China

President of the Supreme People's Court and concurrently President of the Special Court: Jiang Hua

Vice-Presidents: Wu Xiuquan, Zeng Hanzhou and Huang Yukun

Judges: Wang Wenzheng, Wang Zhidao, Wang Zhan-

233

ping, Gan Ying, Shi Xiaotan, Ning Huanxing, Situ Qing, Qu Yucai, Zhu Lizhi, Ren Chenghong, Ren Lingyun, Liu Liying, Liu Jiguang, Xu Zongqi, Yan Xinmin, Su Ziheng, Wu Baosan, Li Minggui, Li Yi, Wu Maosun, Shen Jian, Zhang Shirong, Zhang Min, Fan Zhi, Fei Xiaotong, Luo Tongqi, Gao Chaoxun, Gao Bin, Huang Liangchen, Cao Lizhou and Zhai Xuexi

This copy has been verified and found to be identical with the original.

January 25, 1981

Recording clerks: Guo Zhiwen and Huang Linyi

(Subheads and boldface are ours. — Ed.)

Special Court starts trial of Lin-Jiang cliques, Nov. 20.

The ten principal accused.

被告人

Chief of the Special Procuratorate Huang Huoqing.

President of the Special Court Jiang Hua.

DEFENDANTS

Jiang Qing

Zhang Chunqiao

Yao Wenyuan

Wang Hongwen

Huang Yongsheng

Wu Faxian

Li Zuopeng

Qiu Huizuo

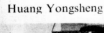

Former State Chairman Liu Shaoqi's widow, Wang Guangmei (*2nd from left*), in the public gallery.

He Long's widow, Xue Ming (*right*), and Lo Ruiqing's widow, Hao Zhiping (*left*), in the public gallery. Their husbands were victimized by the Lin-Jiang cliques.

Chen Boda

Jiang Tengjiao

Where the trial was held.

-First Tribunal chief judge Zeng Hanzhou questioning Jiang Qing.

First Tribunal panel of judges. Fei Hsiao Tung (*1st from right*), author of the preface to this book.

Documents bearing Jiang Qing's approval framing Liu Shaoqi, his wife and others.

Liu Shaoqi's cook, Hao Miao, giving testimony against Jiang Qing.

Widow of film director Zheng Junli, Huang Chen, recounting how Jiang Qing persecuted her husband to death.

Liao Mosha, famous writer, recounting how Jiang Qing persecuted him and others.

Jiang Qing standing trial.

Celebrated jurist Zhang Youyu (*centre*) in the public gallery.

Accomplice Xu Jingxian from Shanghai giving testimony.

Kuai Dafu, former Qinghua University student "rebel" leader, testifying.

Accomplice Wang Xiu-zhen giving testimony.

Zhang Chunqiao in the dock.

Conspirators' arms captured
in Shanghai.

Wang Hongwen in the dock.

Yao Wenyuan in the dock.

Yao Wenyuan's defence lawyers.

Chen Boda's defence lawyers.

Lu Ying, former editor-in-chief of *People's Daily* and a follower of the Gang of Four, testifying.

Defendant Chen Boda.

The demagogic editorial "Sweep Away All Monsters and Demons" revised and approved by Chen Boda.

Wu Xiuquan (*left*), chief judge of the Second Tribunal.

Defendant Jiang Tengjiao standing trial.

Jiang Tengjiao's defence lawyers.

Lin Biao's handwritten order for the coup.

9

Defendant Huang Yongsheng.

Defendant Wu Faxian.

Defendant Li Zuopeng.

Defendant Qiu Huizuo.

Equipment intended for the coup.

Wu Faxian's defence lawyers.

Li Zuopeng's defence lawyers.

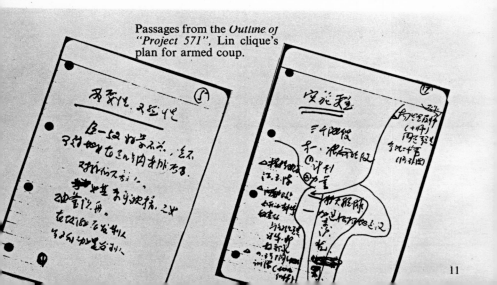

Passages from the *Outline of "Project 571"*, Lin clique's plan for armed coup.

1.

2.

4.

Accomplices of Lin Biao giving testimony in court:

1. Li Weixin (*top left*) who tried to flee in a helicopter.

2. Zhou Jianping, one of the plotters for the assassination of Chairman Mao (*centre*).

3. Lu Min, bomber pilot and hit-man (*right*).

4. Liu Shiying, member of the "Joint Fleet".

Wreckage of the Trident 256 found in Undur Khan, Mongolia.

历 史 的 审 判

*

新世界出版社出版
1981年2月第一版
编号：（英）17223—108
00170
17—E—1564P

⑯